THE DNA OF SAFETY COACHING

A Guide to Empowering People to Achieve Safety and Performance Excellence

By Larry Pearson, Keith Owen and Ron Mundy

Note for Librarians: A cataloguing record for this book is available from Library
and Archives Canada at www.collectionscanada.ca/amicus/index-e.html

ISBN   Soft Cover – 978-1-77084-147-5
         Hard Cover – 978-1-77084-148-2

Printed in Canada
on recycled paper

Contents

The DNA of Safety Coaching

The DNA of Safety Coaching is intended as a guide to help you perform your role as leader/coach more effectively. This book will help you understand why coaching is a requirement of being a great leader. It will explain in clear and simple language what your primary responsibility as leader/coach is (to help people meet their needs and stay safe) and what you need to be able to do to make this possible (to enable people to learn and grow). It will also explain how to prepare for and deliver safety coaching. Finally, it will explain how you can create an environment in which sustainable safety excellence can be achieved.

The book is divided into five parts:

Part 1: THINKING About Coaching

THINKING about Coaching introduces you to some basic ideas and building blocks about coaching. It introduces you to the important role of coach and presents an argument that no matter your current skill level, you need to become a more effective coach. We will explain why coaching is vital to your personal and professional success as well as to your company's, and we will give you a definition of coaching that will serve as a guide to developing your personal coaching capacity (Chapter 1). In Chapter 2, we introduce the concept of the coaching relationship and provide you with a mental framework for understanding what learning relationships are and the tools necessary for creating them.

Part 2: BEING a Coach

BEING a Coach explains how your way of being a coach impacts the success of your coaching. We introduce you to the dynamics of behavioral style in Chapter 3 and explain how it impacts your success as a coach. We also show you how you can develop the flexibility you will need to maximize your success as a coach. In Chapter 4, we introduce you to the basics of adult motivation and learning and how to use this knowledge to make you a better coach. First, we look at the three needs common to all employees and what has to happen for them to meet their needs at work. Next, we look at the conditions you have to create in order to enable your employees to learn.

Part 3: DOING Coaching

DOING Coaching shows you the basic steps required to prepare for and deliver quality coaching. Chapter 5 introduces you to the STEER model of coaching which explains in clear and simple steps how to teach your employees the skills they need to stay safe. Often an employee has a problem that is not caused by a lack of knowledge or skill, but is due to a poor attitude or misguided belief. Chapter 6 shows you how to GUIDE employees to developing healthier, safer beliefs and attitudes.

Part 4: HAVING a Safety Culture

A major concern regarding safety is sustainability. What can you do to ensure you achieve sustainable safety excellence? The answer to this question revolves around the concept of culture.

HAVING a Safety Culture provides a framework and tools for creating a culture in which no incident/no one gets harmed is a way of life. Specifically, we discuss how you can create an environment in which sustainable high performance is possible (Chapter 7). Chapter 8 provides you a brief overview of the key ideas from each of the preceding chapters in the book. This chapter is a distillation of the knowledge and skills you will need to master in order to be a master safety coach, one in which coaching is a way of life.

Part 5: The BASICS for Those in a Hurry

The BASICS for Those in a Hurry contains a description of a variety of tools we have worked with over the years that will assist you in being the best coach you can be. Chapter 9 describes these tools. You can obtain physical copies of each tool by visiting one of our websites (www.ThePearsonGroup.ca or SafetyLeadersGroup.com) and clicking on the Coaching Resources icon. This will enable you to purchase, print, or copy the tools you need and put them to use in your practice.

Introduction

Our acts can be no wiser than our thoughts;
our thinking can be no wiser than our understanding.

GEORGE CLASON

Background

This is a book about being a safety coach. Its aim is to share with you ideas and practices essential to understanding what a safety coach is, what they do and how they do it. This book is based on our 20 plus years of experience in coaching and teaching others how to be effective coaches. What we have learned about coaching is that it is not about teaching employees how to follow a set of safety rules and procedures. What it is about is creating a culture in which people are committed to safe action and who act safe because that is what they want and choose to do.

While this may seem like a fine distinction, it is not. This distinction lies at the heart of understanding how to create an organization in which No Incident/ No One Gets Hurt is the way things are. To put you on the path toward understanding we must start at the beginning and discuss the difference between behavior-based safety (ie. rules) and values-based safety. This is the broad aim of the introduction.

Objectives

By the end of this section you will:

- Understand the difference between behavior-based safety and values-based safety.
- Understand why values-based safety is superior to behavior-based safety.
- Choose to commit yourself to learning the DNA of Safety Coaching.

Behavior-Based Safety versus Values-Based Safety

Let's start by defining the terms.

Behavior-Based Safety (BBS) is an approach based on three things:

Safety rules and procedures - designing safety into the systems and processes and then defining safety protocols for each step in the process.

Education - teaching people how to behave safely.

Enforcement - rewarding correct behavior and extinguishing incorrect behavior.

Values-Based Safety (VBS) is an alternative approach to safety. It is based on the three concepts of behavioral-based safety but is expanded to include three additional concepts:

Empowerment - giving each person the authority and responsibility to improve safety and reduce risk.

Commitment - safety is achieved not through compliance but through choice. Commitment is a belief that something (i.e., no one gets hurt, everyone goes home in one piece every day) is worth striving for. This means that there is a passion for safety that leads people to go the extra mile to ensure that, in fact, everyone goes home safe every day.

Caring - in a values-based culture, the organization cares for its' people and its' people care about the organization.

There is a vast difference between the two approaches and these are highlighted in Table 1. One of the main differences between the two approaches is that in VBS control of safety is internal rather than external. In an internally controlled process, control is based on the principles of self-governance rather than on compliance; in a self-governing process, safety is based on an internal commitment to perform safely. This is the difference between have to and want to and in a self-governing system, people perform safely because they want to, not because they have to.

What difference does this make? It turns out that in values-based safety processes, in contrast to behaviorally, rules-based processes, safety performance is sustainable. In a values-based safety organization, there are fewer accidents and lost time incidents than in a comparable rules-based safety organization. In a values-based safety organization, it is highly likely everyone goes home unhurt each and every day while this is not the case in a behavior-based safety organization.

Table 1: Behavior-Based Safety versus Values-Based Safety

Behavioral-Based Safety	Values-Based Safety
Rules centered	People centered
Control is external	Control is internal
Control is based on compliance	Control is based on commitment
Antecedents trigger behavior	Expectations and choice trigger behavior
Extrinsic motivation	Intrinsic motivation
Acquiescent compliance	Self-governance
Accountability is external	Accountability is a personal responsibility
Closed	Transparent
Objective and observable	Subjective and values-based
Perception and attitude are not important	Perception and attitude are critical
Based on rules	Based on principles
What is everything	Why is everything
Focuses on behavior	Focuses on the whole person
Management	Leadership
Paternalistic	Caring and stewardship
Top down	Empowerment

Behavioral-Based Safety	Values-Based Safety
Focused on fault finding	Focused on fact finding
Individuals to blame	Systems/operations flawed
Outcome oriented	Process oriented
Failure based	Success based
Root cause analysis	Full dimensional analysis

The fundamental distinction between the two views can be summarized in two opposing ideas, which are really distinct world views: COP versus ACE. BBS is based on a COP world view: Control, Order, Prescribe. VBS is based on an ACE world view: Acknowledge, Create, Empower. In the former, people act safe because they have to. Their behavior is governed (controlled) by rules that have been put in place to tell them what to do, when to do it, how to do it and what happens if they don't comply. Consequences are determined by the success with which they follow the rules. In an ACE organization, people act safe because they choose to; they value doing the right thing and find reward in doing so. Their behavior is controlled by the values they are committed to and their actions flow from these values.

COP and ACE organizations are as different as night and day. Behavior-based safety activates compliance and conformity. In COP organizations, people become disengaged when they live and act in a rules-based culture. Values-based safety activates and initiates self-motivation. In ACE organizations, people become fully committed to and engaged in safety as a way of life. Every individual cares about and feels empowered to making the work place safe. In other words, values-based safety activates and motivates both personal responsibility for safety and the power and desire to make a difference.

Values-Based Safety is about You

The most important question you need to ask is not how to coach but why you would want to in the first place. Why does it matter to you? Regarding safety coaching, the issue is not how to act safe but to understand why it matters so deeply. Asking how before understanding why underscores our own doubts as to the possibility of even achieving a safe culture. The challenge of values is not to underscore their relative importance but to act on them.

There is a book titled "The Answer to How Is Yes". Its author, Peter Block, states the case for understanding the riddle. He says, and we agree, that to create a safe work place, you must answer seven questions:

1. What problem have I been postponing? What issue have I been avoiding? Safety just doesn't happen – you have to make it happen.

2. What commitment am I willing to make? A commitment is believing in something so much that you are willing to act like it is true before it is true. Are you willing to act like No Incident/No One Gets Hurt is absolutely true?

3. What price am I willing to pay? What are the moral and ethical costs of doing nothing? Values-based safety requires that you change your behavior from where you are to one who understands and believes in the power of empowerment.

4. What is my contribution to the problem (improved safety) I am concerned with? It is true even if we don't want to admit it – what we see in our group is what we have created as a leader. How does your current behavior contribute to unsafe work?

5. What is the crossroad at which I find myself at this point in my work? If you are not willing to commit to safety now, when will you?

6. What do we want to create together? What is the vision we want to make a reality? What has to happen for you to create in your work place No Incident/No One Gets Hurt?

7. What are the questions that, if you had the answers, would set you free? What are the compromises you have been making? What do you need to start doing and stop doing in order to achieve a No Incident/No One Gets Hurt organization?

The most important principle presented in this book is that coaching is your yes response to eliminating risk in your work place.

To become the best coach you can be requires that you:

- Care about your own role in the safety performance of your group.

- Observe what you are not doing so that you can understand the commitment you must make to become the values leader in your group.

- Analyze the situation so that you can understand the price you must pay to create a values-based culture.

- Communicate this learning and these principles to your group.

- Help them succeed by empowering them to be an important, valued member of the team.

Part 1: THINKING About Coaching

Chapter 1:
Understanding What Coaching Is and Why You Need to Coach

Coaches have to watch for what they don't want to see and listen to what they don't want to hear.

JOHN MADDEN

Background

We have been asked on many occasions "Why do I need to coach?" and we realized that we weren't always able to provide a simple answer to this question. Maybe there is no simple answer; however, there are reasons and this chapter provides them. At the most basic level, being an effective coach is an important part of your responsibility as a leader. It is one of the means by which you enable each of your employees to perform to the very best of their ability. The broad aim of this chapter is to engage you in some thought provoking questions that will help you achieve this purpose.

Objectives

By the end of this chapter, you will understand:
- **What coaching is.**
- **Why coaching is vitally important.**
- **What great coaching is like.**

- **What it means to BE a coach.**
- **What the benefits of coaching are to your employees, your organization and your self.**

Understanding the Role of Coaching

What Is Coaching?

The dictionary defines coaching as the process of training another person. This definition does not capture the essence of coaching, so we have expanded it to:

Coaching is the *process of creating an achievement-oriented, relationship-based* endeavor that enables a person to achieve a level of performance they are currently not achieving.

There are several key words in this statement.

A **process** is a systematic series of actions directed to some end. In other words, coaching is a thoughtful, planned process with the aim of helping others learn.

Coaching doesn't happen by accident – it is something you have to **create**. To create means to bring something into existence. In this case, you have to create the conditions in which people are able to learn and have the desire to do so.

Coaching is focused on **achievement**. It is always about doing something better or doing something new. This means that it is constantly stretching the learner and this is not always easy.

Coaching is based on a trusting **relationship**. Trust does not just happen; you have to bring it into existence through the influence of your own character and behavior.

Coaching fosters or nurtures **learning and change**. This means that your employees will be able to do more or less of something as a result of the coaching process.

The metaphor used to describe how intertwined achievement and relationship are is the DNA molecule. The two strands of the molecule represent the achievement and relationship foci of coaching. The words adjacent to the achievement strand reflect the processes involved in learning and growing. The words adjacent to the relationship strand represent the challenges and dilemmas that must be overcome to create a learning relationship. The structure that gives the molecule its stability is represented by the grey bars connecting the strands. This backbone represents the values, understanding and competencies you bring to the coaching situation. All together, these form the DNA of Safety Coaching (see Figure 1.1).

Figure 1.1: The DNA of Safety Coaching

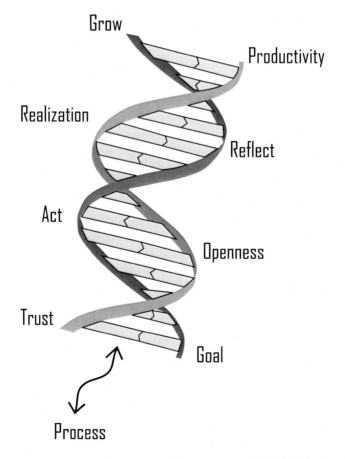

Why is Coaching Important?

In your role as a leader, what enables you to be successful? Isn't it true that your success is utterly and totally dependent on the degree to which your team, individually and collectively, is able to perform its role? This is what leadership is – getting valuable results through the efforts of others.

So ask yourself: Do all your people perform to the best of their ability? Can you delegate responsibility to them with 100% confidence? Does your group achieve total safety? Can they consistently achieve operational excellence?

You probably answered "no" to some or all of these questions, and this is why you need to enhance your coaching skills. In other words, coaching is an essential aspect of your leadership role and practices.

What is Great Coaching?

To gain insight into the answer to this question, think about how confident you would be to leave your team to its own devices in the area of safety. If you have done a great job of creating a culture of safety, you would be totally confident that your team would be able to attain the vision and mission of the group, that they would choose to live the values of the group and that they were essentially self-governing.

In short, you might say your coaching would be considered great if you have created the conditions in which your employees know what safe performance is, know how to perform safely, are committed to performing safety and actually get home safely every evening. You want a self-governing group which chooses to act with excellence in everything it does.

Excellent coaching:

- **Creates an environment in which personal growth and learning are possible and desirable.**
- **Teaches or imparts new knowledge and skills.**
- **Models a commitment to excellence.**

What Does It Mean to BE a Coach?

We like to think of coaching as a way of being in relation to self, others and work. You might be asking, "What the heck does this mean – a way of being"? While it may not be possible to answer this with total clarity, consider the following. Coaching is about caring for others. What do you have to do to care for the growth of another?

Commitment. You must see coaching a particular person as vitally important.

Knowledge and Understanding. To coach, you have to know the other, you must observe them with concentration so that you know what they are doing and what they need to do. You must be committed to this person and willing to follow-up and follow-through.

Courage and Discipline. Coaching takes courage. You must be willing, and have the courage and discipline required, to do the right thing at the right time. Coaching is not giving what you need, but what the learner needs at the time they need it.

Communication and Dialogue. Coaching is primarily a process of engaging the other in dialogue. A dialogue is a two way exchange of information in which both parties agree to a course of action. Coaching is all about change – changing self-perception, understanding, attitudes and action.

Coaching is a way of engaging others. It is a conversation, a dialogue, whereby the coach and the individual interact in a dynamic exchange to move the individual forward to greater success.

What Are the Benefits of Coaching?

The development of people is the responsibility of everyone. It is something that is critical to long term success.

When work is focused on continuous learning, the following results have been achieved:

- **Improved job satisfaction/morale.**
- **Enhanced open communication.**
- **More effective learning.**

- Greater empowerment/teamwork.
- More prepared to meet expectations.
- "Felt" more a part of the team.
- More informed and knowledgeable about customer's needs and requirements.

This is what coaching enables – continuous learning. Coaching produces an array of benefits, for the coach, for the learner and for the organization.

To the Learner, Coaching:

- Improves current performance.
- Develops new knowledge and skills faster.
- Increases self-reliance.
- Increases learning opportunities that direct them towards areas where greatest strengths and interests lie.
- Improves advancement prospects.

To the Coach, Coaching:

- Allows for more effective delegation, saving time and improving team output.
- Ensures building in quality, not inspecting it in at the end.
- Increases the effectiveness of learning that occurs in or close to the customer environment.
- Ensures more responsible, innovative involvement from the team.
- Improves communication and encourages more openness in discussing goals and performance.
- Enhances promotion prospects by having the ability to groom successors.

To the Organization, Coaching:

- Continues to make the professional development and growth of employees a priority.
- Ensures we keep pace as a learning organization.
- Accomplishes higher levels of achievement of organizational objectives.
- Increases the relevancy, efficiency and timeliness of training.

- Increases employee satisfaction.

- Helps people adapt quicker and more readily to the rapidly changing business environment, enabling them to add more value to customers.

- Improves the organization's operational excellence and safety performance.

BEING A Coach

Much of your success as a coach depends on your current way of BEING. This is determined by your core beliefs about people. Do you know what your core beliefs are? To get a feel for this, you might want to use Tool 1.1 – The Core Beliefs Inventory. This tool is described in Chapter 9 and can be found on the Coaching Resources Website at www.coaching-dna.com. This inventory will provide you with clues as to how you tend to perceive and think about others and the effects this pattern of perception has on your way of BEING as a coach.

Chapter 2:
The Learning Relationship

A good coach will make his players see what they can be rather than what they are.

ARA PARASHEGHIAN

Background

The purpose of coaching is to help the learner learn. To facilitate learning, you must first create the conditions under which learning is likely to occur. We refer to these conditions as a learning relationship. The broad aim of this chapter is to examine what we mean by a learning relationship.

Objectives

By the end of this chapter, you will understand:

- **What a learning relationship is.**
- **The four ingredients of a learning relationship.**
- **How you can stretch and expand these ingredients in your relationships.**

Understanding What a Learning Relationship Is

A learning relationship is one which enables (to give the means, competence or ability to) learning to occur. To understand what this relationship looks like, think of a relationship as an emotional involvement or connection between you and the learner. The key here is to think of what is meant by the word emotional. What kind of involvement will create the conditions under which the learner will be receptive to your coaching?

One way to get a handle on this is to imagine that every relationship goes through a series of growth stages. Each stage represents a challenge that can either increase or decrease the learner's receptivity to your coaching efforts. The path along which every relationship grows is illustrated by the terms along the relationship strand of The DNA of Safety Coaching. There you can see the terms Trusting, Opening, Realizing and Inter-Being. Each of these terms represents a step in the evolution of a learning relationship, the final stage of which is Inter-Being, a fancy word for partnership. Since it is at the stage of inter-being that learning takes place, let's look at how you can get there.

Trusting

The first stage of every relationship involves the evolution of trust. Trust is the glue that holds a relationship together and the foundation for how the relationship grows. The dictionary defines trust as the confident expectation of something. In this case, it is the confident expectation of the learner that they can risk exposure to you, that they can be themselves and not be humiliated or rejected. They know they can entrust their weaknesses and insecurities to you and that you will not punish or humiliate them as a result. So the degree to which the learner believes they can trust you resolves an important issue for them – "Will I be accepted?" A confident answer of "yes" paves the way for Opening and for the learning that follows. There are three things you can do to build trust in your relationship with the learner.

Practice transparency or self-disclosure (we call this self-disclosure trust). Self-disclosure is the process of revealing yourself to the learner, telling them straight out what you see, feel and think.

Make sure you keep your commitments and promises (we call this contract trust). If you say you are going to do something - make sure you do it. Also make sure the learner does too.

Protect the learner's physical and psychological safety (we call this safety trust). Make sure the learner knows their safety is of the utmost importance to you.

Opening

Trust is the foundation upon which Opening is built. Opening is the process of laying on the table the things that the learner needs to discover. Opening is like placing a mirror in front of the learner and enabling them to see themselves as they are. In this case, you are the mirror, the eyes through which the learner comes to know their strengths and limitations. The learner's quest for self-understanding is aided by seeing themselves in the mirror that you provide them. It is the learner letting you into their space and willingly accepting your feedback because they know they can entrust this knowledge to you. Opening is what happens when the learner is able to receive your feedback non-defensively.

Realizing

Opening is the foundation for Realizing - the process of setting and achieving behavioral change goals. Realizing starts when the learner is able to see themselves as they are, warts and all, and is able to accept that which they see. They now understand that they are free to learn and change as they choose to. In a relationship based on trust and openness, the learner has no need to defend or protect themselves. This realization opens up the possibility of learning new ways of being and doing. This emerging awareness of possibility leads the learner to discover that they want to learn but not because they think they should or ought to learn. In short, self-realization is possible only when fear has been driven from the relationship. So the degree to which the learner believes they can open up to you resolves an important issue for them – "Can I learn and grow?" In the absence of fear, what's possible becomes evident, as does the courage to create it.

Inter-Being

Realizing paves the way for Inter-Being – which is the state at which you and the learner become partners in the process of learning and growing. The learner comes to realize that success on the job is a collaboration, a coming together of people with shared values and goals and that it is through giving and receiving freedom and fulfillment that the team is able to achieve the goal of total safety. This kind of commitment and effort at work doesn't come from persuasion or rules but from an emerging sense of shared values and commitment to each other. Table 2.1 compares and contrasts such a learning relationship with one we might describe as a defending relationship.

Table 2.1: Learning versus Defending Relationships

Learning Relationship	Defending Relationship	Basic Dilemma
Trusting – Being	Disengaging – Isolating	Trust versus Mistrust
Opening – Showing	Masking – Pretending	Acceptance versus Rejection
Realizing – Growing	Oughting – Shoulding	Fulfillment versus Stagnation
Inter-being – Collaborating	Depending – Obeying	Freedom versus Control

Building the Learning Relationship

The Johari Window is a useful way of thinking about how to build a learning relationship (Figure 2.1). Think of the relationship you have with the learner as a window with four panes. The size of each pane varies in terms of the level of trust in the relationship. The four panes are called the OPEN Area, the HIDDEN Area, the BLIND Area and the UNKNOWN Area.

Figure 2.1: The Johari Window

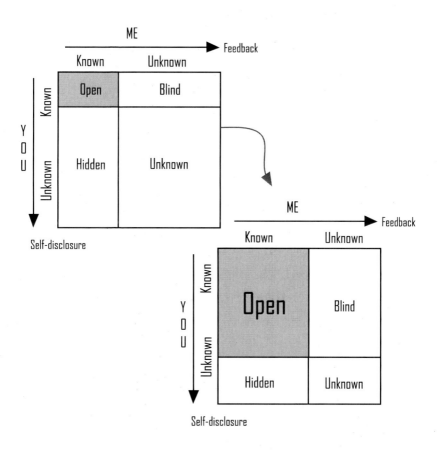

Information that is shared by both learner and coach defines the open area. Information the coach hides from the learner defines the size of the hidden area; information that the learner can see but the coach does not recognize in themself defines the size of the blind area and information that neither knows defines the size of the unknown area. The only information that can be used to learn and grow is that which lies in the open area. The question is – how do you get information into the OPEN Area. The answer to this is simple – you become trustogenic. Table 2.2 looks at how trust levels influence our mind/body processes.

Table 2.2: Trust and the Mind/Body Processes

Mind/Body Process	High trust/Low fear ...	High fear/Low trust ...
Motivation	Creates and mobilizes energy; increases strength and focus of motivation	Energy focused into defensive perception and avoidance behavior
Consciousness	Expands awareness and energy	Reduces span of awareness
Perception	Improves accuracy of perception	Narrows perception
Emotionality	Frees up feelings which then can be used to fuel action	Feelings likely to be defensive and disruptive
Cognition	Focuses thinking and decision making	Thinking and problem solving unfocused, ineffective
Action	Frees up person to engage in proactive behavior	Behavior tends to be reactive and inhibited
Synergy	Increases integration of mind/ body/spirit	Causes disharmony to rule

Practices for Building the Learning Relationship

While there is no magic formula for creating a learning relationship, we have found the following list of practices increases the chances that your relationships with your employees will be learning relationships.

- Be personal and open.

- Get to know your people.

- Engage them in frequent conversations.

- Use questions to find out who they are and what they do.

- Use "I" statements.

- Own your feelings.

- Never blame others for how you feel.

- Be responsible for your reactions to others.

- Share only what can be handled at the time and avoid data dumps.

- Be conscious of your intentions for sharing.

- Be sensitive to the timing of your self-disclosure.

- Contribute to rapport and problem solving.

- Be present; pay attention.

- Concentrate.

- Listen to others.

- Use active listening.

BEING A Coach

Much of your success as a coach depends on how you approach your relationships. Unfortunately, we are often unconscious of our tendencies. Two tools, found on the Coaching Resources Website (www.coaching-dna.com) and described in Chapter 9, will be helpful as you strive to increase your awareness of your typical way of coaching. Tool 2.1 - The TORI Assessment will increase your awareness of these patterns and Tool 2.2 – Effective Coaching Relationships provides you the opportunity to look specifically how effective your current coaching relationships are.

Part 2: BEING a Coach

Chapter 3:
Your Behavioral Style Influences Your Success as a Coach

Make sure that team members know they are working with you, not for you.

JOHN WOODEN

Background

Over a lifetime, each of us develops and exhibits a specific style of approaching situations. Some people become hard chargers, seeking to gain mastery of their environment. Some try to influence and lead others. Some try to fit in and be contributors. Some seek to thoroughly analyze a situation before taking action. This style becomes habitual and we rarely are called on to think about it; however, there are times when we need to assess and evaluate our style to determine how well it is working. Your style impacts your success as a coach. In this chapter, we discuss behavioral style and how your specific style of behavior can impact your coaching. The broad aims of this chapter are to help you understand your style and its impact on your coaching, and to use this understanding to adapt your style so that it is the most beneficial in a given coaching situation.

Objectives

By the end of this chapter, you should:

- Be more aware of your behavioral style.

- Understand how your style impacts the coaching process.

- Have increased flexibility in your behavioral style.

The DNA of Behavior Styles

Born in 1893, William Marston has been credited with developing the first behavioral language called DISC. Educated at Harvard, Marston spent his adult life teaching and consulting psychologists. Marston's early success was in the development of lie detection, but his breakthrough came in 1928 when he published a book, The Emotions of Normal People.

His theory of behavior viewed people along two axes. People tended to behave actively or passively depending on their perception of the environment as either antagonistic or favorable. If you place these axes at right angles, four distinct quadrants are formed with unique characteristics (Figure 3.1):

DOMINANCE produces activity in an antagonistic environment

INFLUENCE produces activity in a favorable environment

STEADINESS produces passivity in a favorable environment

COMPLIANCE produces passivity in an antagonistic environment

Figure 3.1: Understanding The Four Behavioral Styles; D.I.S.C.

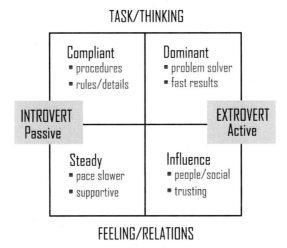

TASK/THINKING

| Compliant • procedures • rules/details | Dominant • problem solver • fast results |

INTROVERT Passive — EXTROVERT Active

| Steady • pace slower • supportive | Influence • people/social • trusting |

FEELING/RELATIONS

During the last century, science has made great advancements in behavioral research, and yet, Marston's theory is still relevant to helping us understand ourselves and others. From the DNA of Safety Coaching perspective, it's easy to see that by understanding the four dimensions of behavior, you can elevate your effectiveness as a coach.

DOMINANCE – CHALLENGE how you approach and respond to problems and challenges as well as how you exercise power.

INFLUENCE – CONTACTS how you interact with and attempt to influence others to your point of view.

STEADINESS – CONSISTENCY how you respond to changes, variations and the pace of your environment.

COMPLIANCE – CONSTRAINTS how you respond to rules and procedures set by others and how you respond to authority.

As a coach, when you consider human behavior there is no right or wrong style. The dominant style is not better than the steady, compliant or influence style. Each style can be a winner in its own right. Each style has the ability to be successful personally and professionally. DISC is a neutral language;

however, are there some characteristics more suited to certain situations? Of course! But each person, once they understand that perspective, can adapt their particular style for maximum impact. By learning and understanding the DISC language, your success as a coach will be greatly enhanced. As a matter of fact, this knowledge will be the most significant factor in determining your level of success as a coach. You will be immersed in a new language of behavior which, if interpreted effectively, will open your eyes to a much greater understanding of those around you.

Predictive Accuracy

In research, the behavioral style assigned to a particular individual proved to be accurate over 85% of the time when the individual responded to the DISC instrument. This is because the DISC language is based on observable behavior. As coaches, when we are observing people, we can easily apply the DISC language if we are familiar with the characteristics of the four factors. Once you begin to recognize the interrelationships of the four factors, your communication effectiveness improves. In order to maximize your effectiveness as a coach, have an in-depth behavioral profile done for you and your team of players. In the meantime, Table 3.1 provides a very effective starting point to understanding the behavioral differences in people.

Table 3.1: Each Style Has Distinct Behavioral Tendencies

Issue	Dominance	Influencing	Steadiness	Compliance
Psychological Need	To direct/dominate others	To interact with others	To serve others	To comply with their own high standards
Predominant Strengths	High ego strength and task oriented	Optimistic and people oriented relaters	Team player, loyal, and supportive of decisions	Accuracy and analysis
Goal Direction	Personal challenges	Social recognition and need to be loved	Traditional practices and harmony	Correct or proper way
Avoidance Goal	Being taken advantage of	Social rejection	Loss of stability	Criticism of their work
Overextensions	Impatience	Disorganization	Possessiveness	Overly critical of self and others

Coaching and Your Behavioral Style

Since coaching is about relating to others, to become the best coach you can be you need to understand your personal style of relating. The goal is not to change your style, for every style has its own unique strengths and weaknesses; however, you do need to understand it so that you can adapt your style to best meet the needs of the situation. Your success at BEING a coach is influenced not only by your behavioral style, but also by your ability to adapt your style to the requirements of the situation.

These preferences, for actively or passively reacting to the environment depending on your perception of the environment as either antagonistic or favorable, affect both your priorities and your pace. Priority refers to your preference for relationships versus tasks. Some people prefer to work with others and involve them in decision making and action, while others prefer to work alone and do things on their own.

Pace refers to your preferences for going fast versus going slow. Your pace can be slow, in between or fast. At the slow end, people prefer to do things in a deliberate, methodical way, carefully thinking through the situation before deciding and acting. At the fast end, people prefer to move quickly – decide quickly and act quickly (see Figure 3.2).

Figure 3.2: The Four Behavioral Styles Expanded

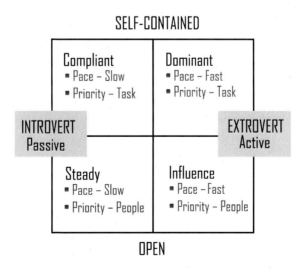

SELF-CONTAINED

Compliant
- Pace – Slow
- Priority – Task

Dominant
- Pace – Fast
- Priority – Task

INTROVERT
Passive

EXTROVERT
Active

Steady
- Pace – Slow
- Priority – People

Influence
- Pace – Fast
- Priority – People

OPEN

What is important for you to realize is that each style is associated with distinctive, easily and consistently observable behavior. Your style is quite clear to others and each pattern has both positive and negative effects on a relationship. For example, the dominant or director type tends to be impatient with themselves and others. This impatience can have a negative impact on your coaching relationships.

In general, your style influences:

- **What motivates you in working with others.**
- **How you make decisions.**
- **How you share.**
- **How you deal with frustration.**
- **How you think about and solve problems.**
- **How you help.**

Increasing Your Flexibility

Your behavioral style impacts both the way you coach and the way others receive your coaching. A key to your success is to learn how to adapt your style to the needs of the coaching situation. We call this Behavioral Flexibility.

Behavioral Flexibility is the skill of using the appropriate style in a given circumstance. You do this by:

- **Understanding your current preferences for priority and pace.**
- **Learning behaviors you do not normally use
  (i.e., learning new styles of relating).**

Your style impacts the way you are, the way you are perceived and the way others respond to your efforts to influence them. Styles are neither wrong nor right; they just are. Still, they are not without an impact.

Your challenge is to:

- **Be aware of your style.**
- **Understand its effect in a given situation.**
- **Adapt it to meet the requirements of the situation.**

Being Aware

You can't change what you don't understand. You can increase your awareness by completing a behavioral profile (see Tool 3.1 – The Behavioral Style Inventory in Chapter 9). You can also increase your awareness by asking others to give you feedback. In any case, each style has its own unique pattern of thinking, feeling and doing. Let's look briefly at some of these patterns.

If You are a D (Dominant)

High D individuals bring many positive attributes to their respective work groups.

Examples of the value they bring include:

- **Bottom-line organizer**
- **Forward-looking**
- **Challenge-oriented**
- **Initiates activity**
- **Innovative**

These tendencies can be offset by the way the D reacts to stress, during which they become:

- **Demanding**
- **Nervy**
- **Aggressive**
- **Egotistical**
- **Angry**

During stressful times, the high D person may exhibit the following limitations:

- **Overstep authority**
- **Set standards too high**
- **Lack tact, diplomacy**
- **Take on many tasks too fast**
- **Impatience with others**
- **Push rather than lead**

The ideal work environment for a high D is:

- **Freedom from controls, supervision and details**
- **An innovative and future-oriented environment**
- **Forum to express ideas/ viewpoints**
- **Non-routine work**
- **Work with challenge and opportunity**

If You are an I (Influence)

High I individuals bring a different set of positives to their respective work groups.

Examples of the value they bring include:

- **Optimism and enthusiasm**
- **Creative problem solving**
- **Motivates others to goals**
- **Team player**
- **Negotiates conflict**

These tendencies can be offset by the way the I reacts to stress, during which they become:

- **Self-promoting**
- **Overly optimistic**
- **Gabby**
- **Unrealistic**

During stressful times, the high I person may exhibit the following limitations:

- **Inattentive to details**
- **Unrealistic people appraisals**
- **Trust people indiscriminately**
- **Situational listener**

The ideal work environment for a high I is:

- **Lots of people contact**
- **Freedom from controls**

- Freedom of movement
- Need to be heard
- A boss that they can be friends with
- Freedom from details

If You are an S (Steady)

High S individuals bring many positive attributes to their respective work groups.

Examples of the value they bring include:
- **Dependable team player**
- **Works for a cause**
- **Patient and empathetic**
- **Logical step-wise thinker**
- **Service-oriented**

These tendencies can be offset by the way the S reacts to stress, during which they become:
- **Non-demonstrative**
- **Unconcerned**
- **Hesitant**
- **Inflexible**

During stressful times, the high S person may exhibit the following limitations:
- **Yields to controversy**
- **Difficulty in setting priorities**
- **Dislikes unwarranted change**
- **Difficulty dealing with diverse situations**
- **Emotionally unavailable**

The ideal work environment for a high S is:
- **Stable and predictable**
- **Environment that allows time to change**
- **Long-term relationships**

- No people conflict
- Freedom from restrictive rules

If You are a C (Compliant)

High C individuals bring many positive attributes to their respective work groups.

Examples of the value they bring include:
- **Maintains high standards**
- **Conscientious and steady**
- **Defines, clarifies, reveals and tests information**
- **Objective – needs reality**
- **In-depth problem solver**

These tendencies can be offset by the way the C reacts to stress, during which they become:
- **Pessimistic**
- **Picky**
- **Fussy**
- **Overly critical**

During stressful times, the high C person may exhibit the following limitations:
- **Defensive when criticized**
- **Bogged down with details**
- **Overly intense for the situation**
- **Somewhat aloof and cool**
- **Fearful**

The ideal work environment for a high C is:
- **Critical thinking is needed**
- **Technical work or areas of specialty**
- **Close relationships, smaller groups**
- **Familiar work environment**
- **Private office or work area**

Understanding Impact

When you interact with others, they make judgments about you based on what they observe. These impressions determine how receptive they will be to your coaching efforts. You can come to understand your impact by reading the feedback provided by the behavioral profile and by observing past coaching efforts. Keep in mind that those you coach also have a style and it influences them just like yours influences you. So, if you are a director type, how do you think another director type will respond to your coaching? The key is to understand your style so that you can achieve a sense of balance (Figure 3.3).

Figure 3.3: To Increase Impact, Strive for Balance

	COMPLIANT	Task	DOMINANT	
	CAN BE– **OFTEN+**		**CAN BE–** **OFTEN+**	
	Critical — Industrious		Pushy — Direct	
	Indecisive — Persistent		Severe — Liberated	
	Stuffy — Serious		Tough — Decisive	
	Picky — Orderly		Intimidating — Efficient	
	Over Analyze — Extensive		Impatient — Results	
Passive				**Active**
	CAN BE– **OFTEN+**		**CAN BE–** **OFTEN+**	
	Conforming — Caring		Manipulative — Ambitious	
	Unsure — Willing		Excitable — Inspiring	
	Pliable — Gracious		Undisciplined — Spirited	
	Dependent — Reliable		Reactionary — Dramatic	
	Slower Moving — Patient		Patronizing — Friendly	
	STEADY	People	INFLUENCE	

Adapting Your Style

You can increase or decrease your openness (task versus people preference) and/or directness (passive versus active preference). Below are some hints for doing so.

Increasing Your Openness (Increasing Your People Focus)

Helps you show/demonstrate greater interest in others:

- Share your feelings more.
- Let people see your emotions and hear your opinions.
- Respond to expressions of feelings by others. Acknowledge their feelings, express selective approval, express understanding.
- Be freer in giving out personal compliments.
- Spend more time with your people.
- Initiate conversations and interactions with your people.
- Be more spontaneous.

Decreasing Your Openness (Increasing Your Task Focus)

Helps you place greater emphasis on tasks:

- Focus more on tasks.
- Establish and keep to your agenda.
- Make your decision based on data.
- Share less of your feelings.
- Be more assertive.
- Set limits and keep them.
- Set clear objectives for each meeting.

Increasing Directness (Increasing Your Pace)

Helps you accomplish more in less time:

- Talk more, ask less.
- Initiate conversations and decisions.
- Give recommendations rather than asking for opinions.
- Take risks.
- Challenge and disagree with others when appropriate.
- Confront others ineffective behavior.

Decreasing Directness (Decreasing Your Pace)

Helps you slow down and get in tune with your employees:

- **Listen more and talk less.**
- **Ask more questions.**
- **Get others involved in decision making.**
- **Refrain from interrupting others.**
- **Use conflict management to handle differences.**

BEING a Coach

As discussed in this chapter, much of your success as a coach depends on how your behavior style is perceived by those you coach. Most of us are not aware of our style, much less its impact. Although we recommend that you do a full DISC™ assessment, Tool 3.1 - The Behavioral Style Inventory provides a quick way to do an assessment of your behavioral style as seen by yourself and others. This tool can be found on the Coaching Resources Website.

Chapter 4: Coaching and Learning

You get the best effort from others not by lighting a fire beneath them, but by building a fire within.

BOB NELSON

Background

A key to your success as a coach is how well you understand why people behave the way they do. While people act to meet their needs, their behavior may not make sense to you. This is because each person develops patterns for meeting their needs that follow their own internal logic and not yours. Understanding this logic makes it much more likely that you will be able to design a coaching strategy for them that works. The broad aim of this chapter is to introduce you to the principles of adult motivation and learning which guide the development of these unique patterns.

Objectives

By the end of this chapter, you will:
- Understand what learning is.
- Understand the three components of motivation.
- Understand how expectations influence learning.
- Understand how to design a learning experience that is engaging and compelling.

Understanding Adult Learning

Background

To get the most from this chapter, we need to introduce you to the concepts of performance and results. Results are the outputs (quantity, quality, timeliness) individuals are expected to produce. Their performance determines the level of results observed. Level of performance is a function of both individual and environmental factors.

Individual Factors and Level of Performance

An individual's level of performance is determined by three things: capability, desire and determination. **Capability** refers to what a person is able to do, **desire** refers to how much they want to do it, and **determination** refers to their willingness to persist even in the face of failure. This is the equipment each of your employees brings to the ball game. Their ability to combine capability, desire and determination is just a potential and their success in doing so is determined by the situation.

Situational Factors and Level of Performance

The situation is performance capable to the extent it provides each employee opportunity, incentive and information. **Opportunity** refers to the job assigned to each person and the clarity with which performance expectations are defined. Incentive refers to the linkage between the results a person produces and the recognition and rewards they receive. **Information** refers to the amount and quality of the feedback each person receives that enables them to compare what they are achieving versus what they need to be achieving.

In the end, your challenge as a coach is to maximize individual potential by maximizing the learning capacity of the environment. To do this you need to have a grasp of what motivates adult learning.

What Is Learning?

The dictionary defines learning as the act or process of acquiring new knowledge or skills, and the relatively permanent modification of behavior through practice, training or experience. So learning is a change in what one knows and/or what one can do as a result of experience, e.g., a coaching lesson.

When you think about how learning occurs, you need to think just a bit about how the mind works. There are several components to the learning process:

Perception and sensory stores. Perception is selectively attending to some of the available stimulation. To get learning to occur, you have to direct the person's attention to specific aspects of the environment. When you do this, however, you must keep in mind that the learner can't learn unless the information you want them to learn gets into his sensory stores. Now, sensory stores have a limited capacity so to increase the person's capacity to store information, it is best if you relate the learning experience to something they already know.

Short term or working memory. When a person first acquires new knowledge or skill, it goes into short term or working memory. This is a temporary way station. What you want is the new information to be transferred to long term memory. This can happen only if the learner is able to rehearse in a meaningful way. The best kind of rehearsal is called active rehearsal, such as when the learner relates a given fact to a larger set of facts or a given skill to a larger process.

Long term memory. If the rehearsal is effective, new knowledge and skills move into long term or permanent memory. You know this has happened when the person you are coaching is able to recall and use the new knowledge and skill. To increase the chances of this happening, it is best if you enable the learner to practice in the context they will be in when they are expected to use the new knowledge and skills. The more they practice in the context, the greater their strength of memory will be. In fact, there is a law expressing the amount of practice and memory strength: Strength = practice, which means the more the learner practices effectively in the context in which they will apply the learning, the more they will learn (or the better he will perform).

There is a difference between what one knows and what one can do and the difference is important to you as a coach. Learning how the world works is referred to as **declarative learning**; learning how to do things to the world is referred to as **procedural learning**. Sometimes you may want to impart knowledge; other times you may want to teach practical application.

Learning and Coaching Strategy

When you coach, the challenge you must overcome is to transfer new knowledge and skills from the learner's sensory store house to their long term memory. You will become more effective at this, of course, as you yourself practice the following general strategy – referred to as the coaching design strategy. This strategy provides a blueprint for just about any coaching you will ever do. It is shown in Table 4.1. The table consists of two columns and five rows. The left column lists the five basic tasks required for learning:

- **Select the information to attend to.**
- **Link the new information with existing information.**
- **Organize the information.**
- **Assimilate the new information into existing knowledge.**
- **Strengthen the new knowledge in memory.**

The right column lists the required elements of most coaching processes, the things that you should build into your coaching plan. It is important that all the elements in a row be included in the coaching to accomplish that particular learning task, however, they need not be accomplished in any particular order as this is determined by the coaching you intend to do.

Table 4.1 - The Coaching Design Strategy

What Learner Must Do	What Coach Must Do
1. Select the information to attend to. Learner must focus on what is relevant and important to their success.	Attention: Focus the attention of the learner. Tell the learner – "What's in it for me" (WIIFM) in the new information? Tell the learner "You can do it" (YCDI) in learning the new information.
2. Link new information to existing information. Learner should put the new knowledge into an existing framework and link it to an existing set of knowledge.	Recall: Bring to the forefront existing (old information) that forms the base upon which new learning will be built. Relate: show similarities or differences between new knowledge and old knowledge so that new knowledge is tied to the old.
3. Organize the information. Learner must organize new knowledge in a way that matches the organization already in mind for related existing knowledge to: Make it easier to learn Cut mental processing Minimize confusion Stress only relevant information	Structure of content: Present the boundaries and structure of the new knowledge in a format that best represents the way the new knowledge itself is structured. Objectives: Specify the new knowledge, values and behaviors to be acquired. Chunking: Organize and limit the amount of new knowledge presented at any one time to match the upper limits of information processing capacity. Layout: Organize presentations in a way that helps the learner organize the new knowledge. Illustrations: Use well-designed illustrations and examples to assist the learner in their organization and assimilation of the new knowledge.
4. Assimilate the new knowledge into existing knowledge. Learner must integrate the new knowledge into the old knowledge so that these combine to produce a new, unified, expanded and reorganized set of knowledge.	Present new knowledge: Using a different approach for each type of knowledge, present the new knowledge in a way that makes it easiest to understand. Present examples: Demonstrate real-life examples of how the new knowledge works when it is expertly applied.

What Learner Must Do	What Coach Must Do
5. Strengthen the new knowledge in memory. Learners should strengthen the new knowledge so that it can be used in the future in new jobs and new situations.	Practice: Involve the learner by having them do something with the new knowledge. Feedback: Let the learner know how well they are doing using the new knowledge. What problems they are having and why? Summary: Present the structure of the new knowledge again including the entire structure of knowledge. Test: Have learner demonstrate the new knowledge to prove to them and you that they have learned. On the job application: Have learner apply the knowledge in a real life situation to ensure they can use it where the rubber meets the road.

Why Do People Learn?

While it is relatively easy to understand what learning is, it is a bit more difficult to understand what you have to do to inspire learning in another. As coach, you have no real direct control over what your employees learn or do not learn. You can't make them learn.

To be a great coach you need to be able to do two things really well:

1. You have to figure out what motivates each person to learn.

2. You have to know how to deliver coaching that fits the need.

People are motivated to learn when it helps them meet their need for achievement, belonging and fairness. When employees are able to meet these needs, they feel good about themselves and their work place; when they are not able to meet these needs, they become apathetic and disengaged from work.

An employee does not always act in ways that help them meet their needs. Every employee develops expectations about how likely it is that if they learn, it will make them more successful at meeting their needs.

As a general rule of thumb, an employee will learn when they:

- **Believe they can learn (Self-Efficacy)**
- **Believe that learning will lead to or produce something of value (Response Efficacy or Personal Control).**
- **Want to learn (Outcome Expectancy or Optimism)**

These three interact to form what is called the motivational triad.

Figure 4.1: The Motivational Triad

How Do Expectations Influence Learning?

It is important to remember this principle: people act according to their expectations. If an employee believes they cannot learn, they can't; if they believe learning won't produce a valued outcome, they won't try; if they believe it won't improve the team's performance, they won't work with a sense of enthusiasm. In fact, expectations can and do act like a self-fulfilling prophecy and consequently, some people get 'addicted' to success while others get 'addicted' to failure. This is illustrated in Figure 4.2. The figure shows that positive or negative, expectations become habitual. Your challenge is to help each employee understand they can learn, that it will produce a valued outcome and that it will make a difference to the team.

Figure 4.2: Expectations are Self-Fulfilling

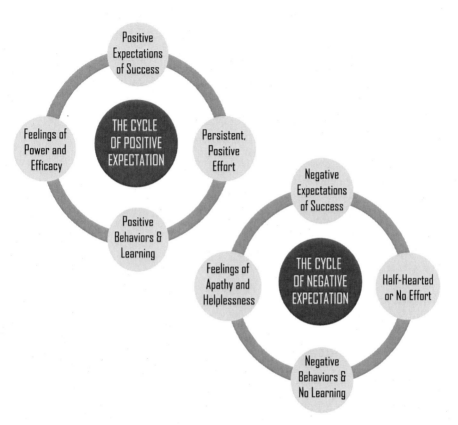

The figure also illustrates that a failure to learn is commonly due to what's called an "expectation problem". An **expectation problem** is unproductive behavior exhibited by an individual who can succeed but who is not currently doing so.

To be an effective coach, you must learn to determine if a given need is caused by a lack of knowledge and skill, or by being caught up in the cycle of negative expectation (Figure 4.3).

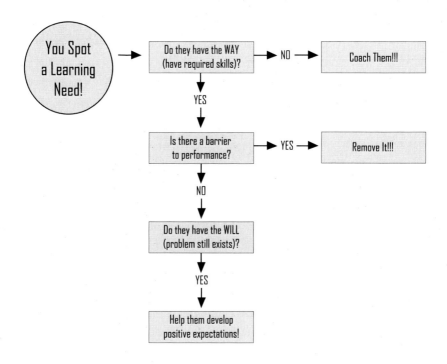

Maximizing Adult Learning

An employees expectations are the most important determinant of if and when they will respond to coaching. Having said this, there are some principles you will want to incorporate into your coaching practices.

Principle 1: People learn when they think they can be successful. Success breeds more success. Strive to arrange the coaching process so that the learner experiences frequent success. This generally means starting with the simplest tasks and progressing towards the most difficult or breaking down a complex behavior into smaller, easier parts.

Principle 2: People learn when it produces a valued outcome. Behavior operates on the environment. A person engages in a given behavior because it produces a predictable outcome. Behaviors that consistently produce a given outcome are repeated over and over and become habits. We call the outcome a behavior produces a reinforcer, which follow the principle of reinforcement. A reinforcement is anything that alters the likelihood of occurrence of a behavior. Reinforcements are often referred to as consequences. So, if you want a behavior to occur more or less frequently, you have to ensure that the behavior in mind is consistently followed by an appropriate reinforcement. There are two classes of reinforcers: positive and negative. While they both work to increase the likelihood a given behavior will occur they do so in different ways, as explained in Table 4.2.

Table 4.2: Types of Reinforcers

Type of Reinforcer	Timing	Effect	Example
Positive	Is given after the proper behavior is exhibited.	Increases the occurrence of a given behavior.	You praise an employee after he does something well.
Negative	Is taken away after the proper behavior is exhibited.	Increases the occurrence of a given behavior.	You decrease the amount of time in study as the person demonstrates increased mastery.

Principle 3: People learn best when their actions make a difference. This might be called the principle of relevance. Adults learn best when they can clearly see how learning will help them grow or how it contributes to the overall performance of the team.

Principle 4: People learn best through practice. This is the repetition principle. Learning requires practice, so you can improve your coaching by ensuring that the learner has many opportunities for practicing the required behaviors.

Principle 5: People learn best through involvement. Adults learn best when they feel a sense of connectedness to their coach. It is important that you get to know the learner and that you also let them get to know you.

Principle 6: People learn best through Doing. This is the engagement principle. People learn best when they have to DO something.

Principle 7: Pace. Learning spread over a relatively long period of time tends to be more effective that learning compressed into a small window of time.

Principle 8: Individualize. Since each learner is more or less unique, you should strive to adapt your coaching style to the learner's style.

Principle 9: Problem Solving. Adults learn best through experience. Set up learning so that the learner has to solve a problem.

BEING a Coach

As we discussed above, expectations are self-fulfilling, even the ones you make about those you coach. This is because we all make assumptions about learners and learning. Tool 4.1 – Assumptions about Learners and Learning found on the Coaching Resources Website will help you think about your assumptions and their impact on your effectiveness as a coach.

Part 3: DOING Coaching

Chapter 5:
Delivering Coaching – The STEER Model

Probably my best quality as a coach is that I ask a lot of
challenging questions and let the person come up with the answer.

PHIL DIXON

Background

The focus in this chapter is on the process of creating behavior change when
the need is in the WAY category, that is, when the learner has the desire but
not the skill to perform their role safely. The broad aim of this chapter is
to show you how to STEER your employees toward increased competence,
commitment and disciplined effort.

Objectives

By the end of this chapter, you will be able to:

- Diagnose a learning need.
- Distinguish between needs stemming from problems with
  the WAY and needs stemming from problems of the WILL.
- Spot a coaching opportunity.
- Tailor your coaching to the learner's style of learning.
- Explain how to perform successfully.

- **Empower to perform successfully.**
- **Recognize and reinforce learning and behavior change.**

Diagnosing the Need

The first challenge of being a great coach is to understand the underlying cause of the need for coaching. In fact, not all 'learning' needs are the same because there are two distinct sides to performance – the WAY and the WILL.

Some needs occur because a person does not know how to do something they would like to do. For example, a given employee would like to behave more safely but they may not know how to in the context in which they are working. This person can be said to have a problem with the WAY. Another employee in the same job and context may know how to behave safely but consistently acts in ways that increase risk. They are motivated to reduce and/or eliminate risk, but are not sure how to. This person knows how to behave safely but is not committed to doing so. This person can be said to have a problem with the WILL.

These two types of problems present different coaching challenges. In the first case the challenge is to help the person learn something new; in the latter case, the challenge is to help the person discover the self-defeating nature of their own attitudes and help them learn and live more positive attitudes. This is not a problem of coaching in the normal way of understanding coaching. This is a problem of helping the learner gain an insight into the self-defeating nature of their actions and helping them understand and accept the fact that they have a choice of doing better and that it is up to them to make that choice. In this case, your role is that of a mirror and your challenge is to help the learner look into it and see what is there and not what they wish were there.

Because there are two sides to performance, your first task as a coach is to spot a need and understand its root cause: the WILL or the WAY. Figure 5.1 provides you a useful tool for making this determination. If a person is willing to perform but can't, your job is to coach or STEER them. If they can perform but are unwilling to do so, your role shifts to that of a GUIDE.

In this chapter the focus is on problems with the WAY (Figure 5.1).

Figure 5.1: Diagnosing a Learning Need

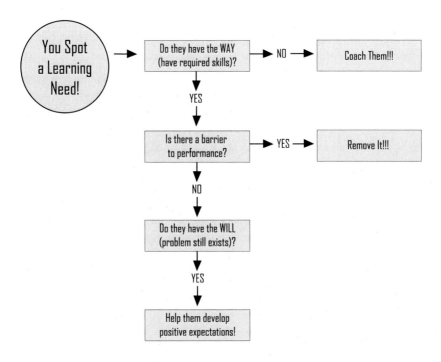

Steering the Learner

The analogy of steering is appropriate for helping the learner see how they can perform more safely. Steering is a verb that means to direct the course of someone. In this case, the aim is to steer the learner's behavior so that they can perform more safely. Figure 5.2 illustrates the basic process of executing STEER. As you can see there are five inter-related processes:

- **Spot the Need**
- **Tailor the Coaching**
- **Explain and Demonstrate**
- **Empower and Encourage**
- **Recognize and Support**

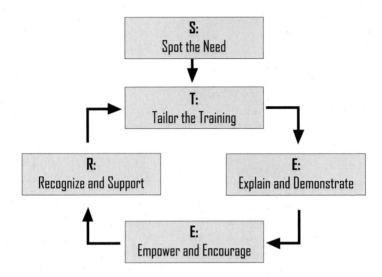

S = Spot the Need

Coaching starts with observation and as you observe your employees you may notice gaps between current and desired (required) behavior. These gaps represent coaching opportunities that are critical to the success of your team.

What You Are After

You want every one of your people to be a winner, an employee who is doing the very best they can do. You want your people to perform competently and safely. It takes knowledge, skill and determination to be a winner. To be a safety winner, each person must understand what safety is on their job, how to perform safely and have the determination to do so.

What It Is

A need is a gap between what is and what should be and the aim of coaching is to eliminate this gap. Your first step is to spot the need and then to understand its origin. Why does the need exist? If the gap is caused by a lack of knowledge and/or skill (the WAY), then STEER the person (Figure 5.3).

Figure 5.3: Understanding the Learning Need

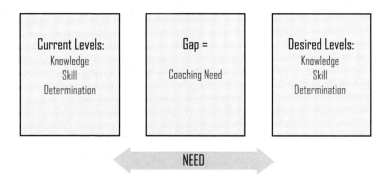

Current Levels:	Gap =	Desired Levels:
Knowledge		Knowledge
Skill	Coaching Need	Skill
Determination		Determination

NEED

How You Do It

Spotting a need is determining where the gaps are and then figuring out how to close them. How do you 'analyze' the need so that you can do so? The key to spotting needs is actually very simple – you have to know what your people are doing. Quality coaching is based on caring, observation, analysis, communication and helping.

Some of the specific behaviors that will help you understand what people are doing are:

- Make sure everyone knows their job description/expectations and how their job fits into the bigger scheme of group and organizational goals.
- Establish performance goals and metrics for each job.
- Establish standards of excellence for each critical job task.
- Observe and pay attention to the learner.
- Make a habit of giving the employee informal feedback, comparing their actual to expected performance.
- If you spot a gap, ask the learner to tell you areas in which they are having difficulties.
- Ask the learner what they need.
- Use questions to identify areas the learner is having trouble with.

T = Tailor the Coaching to the Need and the Person

Every person is unique and no two people can be expected to learn alike. To be the most successful coach possible you need to tailor your coaching to the style and needs of the person you are coaching.

What You Are After

Tailoring involves two things: 1) You need to make sure your coaching fits the learning style of the other; 2) You need to make sure the learning experience fits the need. What you are after is a coaching plan that fits the style and specific needs of the learner. Let's look at each of these.

The Learner's Style of Learning

People learn in one of four different ways (Figure 5.4). Some people are **concrete learners** and rely on hands-on experience. Some learn through **reflection** and learn best by listening and observing. Some rely on **conceptual learning** which means they learn best by first understanding concepts and then operations. Finally, some people learn by **doing** – they learn through trial and error.

By understanding the learner's style, you will be in a better position to tailor your coaching to the person in two ways:

1. You can adjust your coaching so that it is compatible with the way the learner processes information.

2. You can teach the learner to appreciate a need from new perspectives.

Figure 5.4: Learning Styles and the Learning Process

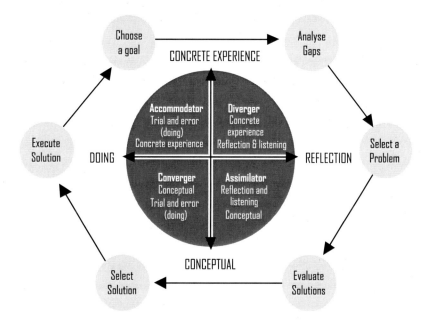

Fit the Learning Experience to the Level of the Need

To perform a given job or task excellently, a learner has to have the knowledge, behavioral skills and attitude. Each of these prerequisites must be taught in a way that is appropriate to it. As you are tailoring your coaching, you have to create a learning activity that is appropriate to the level of the need you are targeting:

- **To meet a Knowledge Need, explain the job/task to the learner.**
- **To meet a Skill Need, demonstrate the job/task for the learner.**
- **To meet an Attitude Need, model the appropriate attitude for the learner.**

What It Is

Now that you understand that each person learns in a different way, you need to use this understanding in developing a coaching plan. A coaching plan is a blueprint or outline of how you intend to deliver the coaching.

A good plan has each of the following:

- **A goal that defines in behavioral terms the specific knowledge, skills and attitudes the learner should be performing.**
- **The standards of excellence you will use to evaluate the behavior.**
- **The learning experiences that you will use to deliver the coaching.**
- **A description of how you will execute each step.**

How You Do It

The key behaviors required to execute this step are:

- **Identify the need and its dimensions or levels.**
- **Observe the learner. How do they seem to learn best?**
- **Tailor the coaching process so that it is appropriate to the learner's style. That is, define experiences that will meet the need at the level of the need.**
- **Develop a coaching plan that specifies what is to be learned in behavioral terms and identifies what resources you will need to implement the plan.**

A sample coaching plan is shown in Tool 5.3 – Developing a Coaching Plan found on the Coaching Resources Website.

E = Explain and Demonstrate the New Behavior

Now that you have your plan, you are ready to execute it. This is the process of explaining, demonstrating and modeling the new behavior.

What You Are After

The aim here is first to describe the task and its relationship to the process/system of which it is part and second to demonstrate how to execute the task(s). Another aim is to allow the learner the time to ask questions and increase their understanding.

What You Are After

What you want to do is model how to perform the task(s) the correct way in a given situation. The correct way of behaving may involve a set of related behaviors so you have to be prepared to explain and demonstrate the behavior in its entirely so make sure you are well prepared.

How You Do It

Whether it is a process that extends over time or a response to a moment of truth, you execute this step by:

- Communicating the need for the coaching and why it is important. Explain the principles you are after and why these are crucial to the value of No Incident/No One Gets Hurt culture.

- Describe the process from start to finish and show the learner how their role fits into the process.

- Tell the learner what to do in relation to the process.

- Show them how to do it. Demonstrate each step of the process and explain the steps as you go along. Point out potential problems.

E = Empower New Behavior

In the end, you want to teach the employee how to act on their own. In short, you want to empower them to perform new behavior. Your task is to make sure the learner is at ease and is focused on learning the task and not on the possibility of failure.

What You Are After

This is where the learner learns. All learning goes through four stages:

- Unconscious incompetence – being incompetent but not aware of it.

- Conscious incompetence – being incompetent and also aware of your ineffectiveness.

- Conscious competence – being competent at a task but having to try to perform effectively.

- Unconscious competence – your execution of a competence has become second nature and you perform without having to think about what to do next.

The aim here is to transform a person from unconscious incompetence to unconscious competence.

What It Is

Empower means to give the authority and the responsibility to do something. Empowerment also encompasses the notion of accountability. When you empower a person, you give them the authority, tools and resources for accomplishing a task. You make them accountable with the understanding that, if they cannot succeed, the natural consequence is to find someone who can.

There is more to empowerment than authority and accountability. There is also the matter of creating an environment in which trust levels encourage risk taking and receptivity to feedback. This is your responsibility as coach – to create an environment of high trust and low fear. The aim is to create an environment in which people behave safely as a matter of principled choice. Keep in mind that this type of learning and behavior will only take place to the extent your workplace is characterized by high levels of trust and openness – a so-called high performance environment. We discuss how you can create such an environment in great detail in Chapter 7.

How You Do It

A few simple steps will help you execute this step successfully:

Make sure the learner is aware of the need you are addressing.

Make sure the learner is comfortable. This might involve making sure the environment is conducive to learning or reassuring the learner that your intention is to make sure they can perform the tasks at hand and stay safe.

Allow the learner to execute the process step by step. Have them explain why and what they are doing.

Provide feedback and encouragement as you go along.

Provide corrective feedback. Feedback is the basis for all learning and growth. By comparing the effects of our actions against our intentions, we can learn more effective responses to our work and life situations. Since feedback is so important, you might want to consider these simple rules for giving feedback:

- It is descriptive of behavior rather than judgmental?
- It is specific and focused rather than general?
- It is directed toward behavior which the receiver can do something about?
- It is well-timed?
- Does it involve sharing of information rather than giving advice?
- Does it take into account the amount of information the receiver can use rather than the amount we would like to give?
- Is it checked to ensure clear communication?

R = Review Progress and Recognize New Behavior

Remember the aim of coaching is to move your people toward unconscious competence, toward a place where they perform at a level of excellence because they want to.

What You Are After

The aim here is to have each learner internalize the values and goals of the group.

For each of your employees, what you are after is:

Competence – the ability to perform in a cost effective manner.

Commitment – the desire to perform.

Congruence – the public choice to live the values of the group.

Engagement – the willingness to go the extra mile to ensure the goal of No Incident/No One Gets Hurt is achieved.

This boils down to creating an internally motivated, committed, responsible, disciplined employee who is self-governing with respect to the values and aims of the group.

What It Is

What you are after is employees who are self-directed and internally motivated to achieve safety excellence. We call this self-governance and this does not just happen. It is something you create on a day to day basis as you establish an achievement orientation based on relationships built on trust and openness. An achievement focus and relationships based on trust and openness are the outcome of your modeling and coaching these values on a day to day, moment by moment basis. This means that on a day to day, moment by moment basis you must care for your group and its individual members, be aware of what each person is doing, analyze what is happening, communicate openly about what you see happening and why and help the group and its members perform better.

How You Do It

The key points in this phase are to:

- Observe the learner as they try to master the new ways of behaving.
- Determine what is going well and what is not going well.
- Ask the learner to reflect on what is working and what is not working.
- Ask them what they think they need to change or alter.
- Provide suggestions as to how they might make their plan more attainable.
- Provide recognition for the things that are going well.
- Provide corrective feedback for the things that are not going well.
- Avoid criticizing or punishing the learner.
- Keep on trying, even if the learner gets discouraged.

Summary

All learning follows a natural cycle (Figure 5.5). It starts with a need and a plan to meet that need. This is followed by a period of doing, of experimentation with new behaviors. This period of experimentation is followed by period of reflection and assessment about what worked and why and what didn't work and why. This reflection is what enables learning. As this figure shows, adults learn best when they are actively engaged in the cycle of learning.

Figure 5.5: Experiential Learning is Best for Most Adults

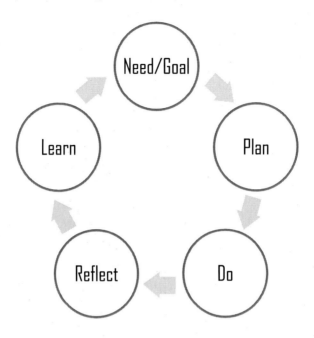

BEING A COACH

To help you STEER behavior, use the tools found on the Coaching Resources Website and described in Chapter 9 - a kit of tools you can use to guide you through each phase of STEER. Tool 5.1 shows you how to spot coaching opportunities; Tool 5.2 helps you diagnose a learning need; Tool 5.3 helps you develop an effective plan for delivering your coaching and Tool 5.4 provides you a series of behavioral checklists you can use to evaluate your coaching from spotting the opportunity to providing recognition.

Chapter 6:
Delivering Coaching – The GUIDE Model

My father gave me the greatest gift anyone could give another person, he believed in me.

JIM VALVANO, BASKETBALL COACH

Background

Here we explore the process of creating behavior change when the need is in the WILL category. The broad aim of this chapter is to show you how to GUIDE the learner toward increased competence, commitment and disciplined effort when the presenting need is not due to a lack of skill but a lack of determination.

Objectives

By the end of this chapter, you will be able to:

- **Understand the GUIDE Model.**
- **Get involved at a personal level.**
- **Use questions to enable understanding of current behavior.**
- **Enable the learner to investigate natural consequences and make new choices about what they want.**
- **Develop a learning plan.**
- **Encourage change.**

Changing the WILL

This chapter continues the requirements for creating behavior change when the need lays in the WILL category. These needs are related to the player's deep-seated expectations and values. The principle underlying the discussion is that each of us chooses our own pathway and that it is not imposed on us by outside forces. In other words, each of us is responsible for the choices we make. Our current path is but the natural consequence of these choices and if we want different consequences, we must make different choices. The aim of this chapter is to show you how to GUIDE the learner towards making better choices, choices that produce more desirable natural consequences.

Expectations and Learning

When one of your employees has difficulty learning or shows resistance to doing so it is often caused not by a lack of knowledge and/or skill, but by negative expectations. Expectations reflect an individual's basic beliefs about what is important, what they perceive as opportunities and what they perceive as reality. Such beliefs shape what a person expects to get from learning and thus determine the person's thoughts, feelings and behavioral choices.

The Expectation Cycle

Whether the expectations are positive or negative, behaviors tend to conform to them. This is because expectations act like a prophecy. If you expect to be successful, you tend to act like a successful person would act. If you expect to be a failure, you tend to act like a failure would act. As odd as it may seem, people become addicted to success or failure and the quality of their addiction is determined by their expectations. Your challenge as a coach is to change this cycle; and herein lays the rub; it is not possible for you to do so. This power is the domain of the learner. Only they can change the cycle of expectations. Your role is to bring the learner to a point where they are able and willing to do this.

Prerequisites of Change

Your ability to bring the learner to this point of re-decision is enhanced if you think about the four conditions that are necessary for change on the personal level:

A state of dissatisfaction with current affairs. An employee who needs to learn new attitudes is feeling dissatisfied because their behavior is producing negative consequences. There is a gap between actual and required performance and this is uncomfortable for them.

A vision of a better way of being. The person who is confronted with the need to make a life changing choice must have a view of a better way of being. Your role is to help the learner see this new reality.

A structure within which change can take place. A person cannot think their way out of a behavioral hole; they must walk out one step at a time. However, they have not been able to do this in the past so your responsibility as a coach is to provide the structure of a relationship with you that is based on trust and openness. We call this a learning relationship.

The power to make change happen. To perform, each person must have the ability, opportunity and desire to do so. As coach, you help the learner understand that they already have each of these.

GUIDING Change

GUIDE is a process (Figure 6.1). For ease of explanation we have broken it down into five inter-dependent steps:

G = Getting Involved. This is the process of creating a learning relationship.

U= Understanding Current Behavior. The learner's pain is embedded in their choices and these choices are revealed in their behavior. Together, your role is to help the learner explore these behaviors and their consequences.

I = Investigate Consequences. Every choice produces a natural consequence. Together, you and the learner explore these consequences. Additionally, you guide the learner to decide if these consequences are what they want.

D = Develop a Plan. If the learner decides they want better consequences, you and the learner develop a plan to produce them.

E = Encourage and Support the Change. Change doesn't take place overnight. It is the outcome of a long term commitment. Your role is to help the learner develop a commitment and responsiveness to the plan.

Figure 6.1: The GUIDE Model; Dealing with the Will

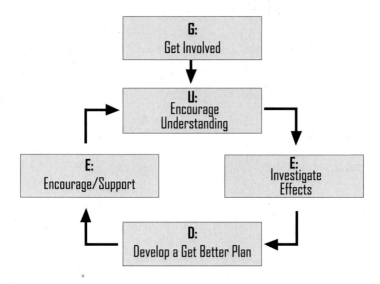

G = Get Positively Involved

Getting involved is establishing a level of trust that frees the learner to open up and reveal themself to you. The aim of this step is to establish a level of personal involvement and to build a level of trust that frees the person to tell you truthfully and openly what is happening.

What You Are After

What you are after is a learning relationship. This is a special kind of relationship in which the person you are engaged with allows you to influence them by choice and not because they are afraid of you. In this kind of relationship, the other person chooses to receive your feedback openly, to reflect on it and to incorporate it into their behavior.

What It Is

A learning relationship is one in which the other person is open to your influence and leadership. Their receptivity to your influence is built on a foundation of trust. Trust means the learner feels confident that you will do what you say you are going to do and that you will and do speak the truth to them. It is the involvement in this kind of relationship that people learn and grow.

A learning relationship has four defining qualities – Trust, Openness, Realization and Collaboration. These four qualities are part of the system that is the relationship and from this fertile ground comes the possibility of learning and growing, for this is what people do when they are freed to do so.

How You Do It

There are several things you must do to establish positive involvement.

- **Let the learner understand your intentions. Be transparent to the learner. Being transparent is achieved through the quality of your self-disclosure. It is sharing what you are thinking and feeling in the moment.**

- **When you make the decision to share what you are feeling and experiencing, you are practicing constructive openness. To practice constructive openness:**
  - Let it evolve out of the relationship itself.
  - Use "I" messages to describe your experiences; avoid starting messages with "You".
  - Stay in the here and now (present moment awareness), sharing what is relevant in the present.
  - Be as specific as possible in describing what you are experiencing and what you want.
  - When solving problems, offer alternatives, not solutions.
  - Avoid criticizing, blaming and other forms of non-talk.

- **Assume full responsibility for stating your feelings and wants. You can improve communications by:**
  - Asking the listener to paraphrase what you have said.
  - Clarifying any misperceptions.

- **Make sure you always do what you say you are going to do.**
- **Take an active role in seeking to understand the learner.**
  The effective use of questions:
  - Establishes an engagement mind set.
  - Clearly states interest in the subject.
  - Clarifies any situation.
  - Creates a transparent, inclusive communication environment.
  - Forces people to think.
- **Ask good questions. Asking good questions is not about conducting an interrogation or having a therapy session. It's about creating a conversation where you are genuinely interested in hearing what the other person (the learner) has to say. If you aren't sure where to begin, start by asking a question that you think you know the answer to. If there is a difference between what you thought and what you are told, you'll have a better idea of the scope and importance of the problem.**

U = Understand Current Behavior

Current dissatisfaction (the need) is the natural consequence of a person's choices. These choices are revealed in a person's behavior. To understand these choices, you must help the learner explore their current behavior.

What You Are After

The aim here is to help the learner understand that their pain is self-induced, that this pain is the natural consequence of their choices and the actions that follow these choices. In other words, you want to create a level of dissatisfaction in the learner that will motivate them to change. At the same time, you want to show them there is a way out of the mess they are in.

What It Is

A person's problems are always revealed in the choices they make and the actions they take. For example, a person who has time management issues is usually late and if not late, unprepared. This step takes the learner on a personal journey towards awareness that their pain is the natural consequence of their behavioral choices. The word "natural" means that the cost of a given behavior is the logical outcome of a given set of choices. This awareness enables the person to begin to feel as if they have control over what they experience and that this control is a natural consequence of their choices.

How You Do It

Help the learner explore what they are doing. Use questions to guide the learner in making this discovery.

- **When do you get to work?**
- **How do you prepare for the day?**
- **How much sleep did you get?**
- **What did you eat for breakfast?**

As soon as you feel you understand how they use their time during a typical day, help the learner talk about the results they are getting on the job. Obviously, you would not be involved in the process of GUIDING them if their behavior were exemplary. Again, the judicious use of implication questions is the way you do this:

- **What happens when you ....?**
- **What will happen if you continue to ... ?**
- **What will the effects of ... be on your job?**
- **What will be the financial / personal impact be of... ?**

When you feel confident that the learner understands the results they are getting and their natural consequences, engage them in an exploration of the mental models (beliefs and expectations) that underlie these results. Again, learning to question is very important:

- **What do you think about these results?**
- **What kinds of assumption do you think underlie your thoughts? e.g., What is your attitude about the results? Can you control them? Do you believe the way you think has an effect on the results you are getting?**
- **What is it that you seem to believe about yourself and your work that produces the results you are getting?**
- **What will be the long term results if you keep on thinking in this manner?**

- **Are you satisfied with these results or would you prefer to produce different results?**

- **Do you believe you can do things differently?**

Coaches need to continually work on their questions. The critical point is to always be objective and commit to getting to the root of the issue or problem. Develop and deliver your questions in such a fashion that you always maintain a level of control without any aggressive positioning or hostility. Consider the following strategies and tactics to help you stay focused and keep the coaching conversation on the right track.

Think win/win – Questions are not designed to beat someone or push him or her into a corner. Your goal is to make the learner as comfortable as you can. Clarify with additional questions that the learner heard you and they understand the purpose of your questions. Ask questions that help the learner understand their options, other points of view and what they could do differently. Your challenge is to stay as neutral as possible.

Control the pace – Don't ask questions so quickly that the learner thinks they are being cross-examined. A simple conversational approach can diffuse potential uncomfortable situations, ease any tension that may exist and establish a connection. Remember that questions provoke both thought and emotion, and the higher the emotion the lower the listening. Control the pace of questioning so the learner can think clearly and give honest responses.

Be observant – You may not have the skill to fully recognize when someone is lying or trying to hide something; however, everyone can recognize clues when a question strikes a chord within the other person. How they respond is a sure giveaway. Be observant to the following clues:
- Widening of the eyes or they look away quickly.
- Speech pace changes quickly or they go from talking softer to louder.
- Breathing changes, faster or slower.
- Their body language sends messages, folding the arms tightly or gestures openly and often.
- Their body position changes, away perhaps fearful or more assertive toward you.

Plan questions – Prior to any coaching session, take 5 minutes alone and reflect on the questions you will ask during your time with the player. We don't advocate that your session be canned, without flexibility; however, we have found that any coaching sessions' effectiveness is greatly improved with a series of planned, well thought out questions.

Stay focused – Understanding the characteristics of each behavior style will enhance your ability to stay focused. When developing your questions, consider the learners style. Will the question spark their thought process or will it come across as dull and of little value. Good questions also support the coach and their ability to stay focused. A good plan of attack will help keep your head in the game.

Engagement - Questions should be simple yet logical and should be asked politely. The real key is engagement. When asking questions, they need to be asked from the other person's perspective.

I = Investigate the Consequences of Current Behavior

The aim of this step is to help the learner discover that the current dissatisfaction is the natural consequence of a person's choices. You do this by focusing the learner's attention on the consequences of their actions.

What You Are After

Your aim is to bring the learner to a place that they can see the relationship between their choices and the consequences they are experiencing and that they have the power to make different choices. This realization is the first step on the way to becoming more responsible and accountable for one's own actions.

What It Is

Responsibility for the consequences of one's actions is an important step towards personal maturity and integrity. Responsibility is accepting the reality that choosing path A creates the current pain they are experiencing, choosing path B leads to personal gratification, and that which path they take is entirely up to them. This step is all about learning how to live one's values.

Figure 6.2: Don't Punish, but Allow Natural Consequences

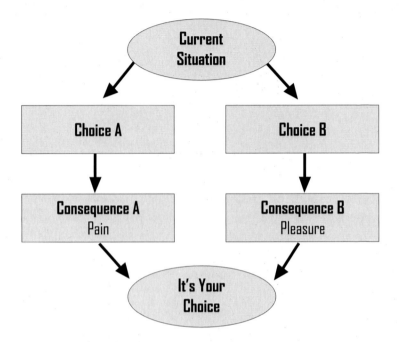

How You Do It

When you feel confident the learner understands the results they are getting and their natural consequences, engage them in an exploration of the beliefs and expectations (mental models) that underlie these results. Again, learning to question is very important:

- **What do you think about these results?**
- **What kinds of assumption do you think underlie your thoughts, e.g., what is your attitude about the results? Can you control them? Do you believe the way you think has an effect on the results you are getting?**
- **What is it that you seem to believe about yourself and work that produces the results you are getting?**

- What will be the long term results if you keep on thinking in this manner?
- Are you content with these results or would you prefer to produce different results?
- Do you believe you can do things differently?
- When you feel as if the learner understands they have a choice in how they feel, help them explore new ways of being.
- What are some new ways you might behave?
- Have you thought of ....?

D =Develop a 'Get Better' Plan

A plan is the learner's blueprint for success. The aim of this step is to help the learner develop a plan that will be successful.

What You Are After

Once the learner understands what the consequence of continuing along their current path is, and that there are positive alternatives, it is time to move them along the path toward responsible self-discipline. It is time to help them get better by changing their behavior. Responsible self-discipline is the awareness that one is responsible for their choices and their consequences and that it takes committed effort to change these choices and experience different consequences.

What It Is

The learner learns by developing a 'Get Better' plan. A plan is just a blue print that helps the learner make the right choices about what they should be doing on a day to day basis. Changing an attitude is no simple matter, however. It took a long time for the learner to develop attitudes that are self-limiting (and in some cases self-destructive) and it therefore takes a long time to learn more positive attitudes. This is where a good learning plan comes into play. It provides the structure the learner requires in order to learn responsible self-discipline.

How You Do It

A good 'Get Better' Plan:

- Is simple enough to ensure initial success.
- Is a DO plan rather than a stop doing plan.
- Is non-contingent; dependent on the learner's choices and actions and not on others.
- Is a NOW plan, something that can be started immediately.
- Is specific.
- Requires a commitment.
- Requires effort.

A sample get better plan can be found in Chapter 8.

E = Encourage Learning

Changing almost always involves failure. The aim of this step is to create a haven where the learner can remain motivated to succeed even in the face of failure and setbacks. The broader aim is for you to let the learner know that you are going to keep trying and that you want them to do the same.

What You Are After

There can be no learning without failure and since some failure is inevitable as the learner strives to develop new, more self-fulfilling attitudes, it is up to you to act as the buffer to their natural tendency to give up and quit. Not only must the learner be responsive to their plan, you must be responsive to the learner's effort to do the plan.

What It Is

The word hospice is defined in the dictionary as a house of shelter. In a symbolic sense, you must build and maintain this house of shelter for the learner as they take the journey to reduce the gap between their current results and future results.

How You Do It

You help build and maintain this 'learning shelter' by:

- **Frequently following up on the plan.**
- **Evaluating results but avoiding blame or criticism.**
- **Providing correct feedback. Again using questions judiciously will prove very helpful:**
  - · What worked well for you?
  - · What didn't work?
  - · Was the plan a good one?
  - · If not, what do you think the flaw was?
  - · Was it in your control?
    If no, what can we do to make it more controllable?
  - · Was it simple enough to ensure initial success?
    If no, what can we do to simplify it?

SUMMARY

GUIDE involves a journey on which you and learner form a learning partnership. Through involvement, you and the learner explore the pain and dissatisfaction of current reality and co-create an alternative, more gratifying possible reality. However, GUIDE works only to the extent that the learner knows that you will stay the course and not give up on them prematurely for this is what the learner already knows how to do much better than you.

BEING A COACH

To help you GUIDE attitude change, use the tools found on the Coaching Resources Website and described in Chapter 9. This is a packet of tools that will help you though the GUIDE process. Tool 6.1 shows you how to spot attitudes that need changing; Tool 6.2 helps you diagnose a need; Tool 6.3 helps you evaluate your "GUIDING" skills; Tool 6.4 guides you in developing a get better plan with the learner; and Tool 6.5 provides you a series of behavioral checklists you can use to evaluate your guiding from being open and transparent to providing encouragement.

Part 4: HAVING a Safety Culture

Chapter 7:
The High Performance Environment

*The best teacher is the one who suggests rather than dogmatizes
and inspires his listener with the wish to teach himself.*

EDWARD BULWER-LYTTON

BACKGROUND

Coaching always takes place in a specific work or organizational environment.
We call this environment the context. Each work environment requires those
that work there to use a particular set of knowledge, skills and values at a
particular level of mastery to perform the tasks they are expected to perform.
In a high risk work environment, it is absolutely essential that each person
perform certain tasks at a level of excellence. Each person's commitment and
willingness to learn to perform at this level is not an accident, but the outcome of specific leadership practices and also the broader context in which
the work takes place.

A No Incident/No One Gets Hurt environment is possible only to the extent
that you can develop values-based self-governance. We referred to this as an
ACE mentality. Values-based self-governance is possible only when every one
of your people are fully committed to the values and goals of the group and
110% motivated to be successful at achieving total safety. Such an environment is high trust and low fear. In such environments people act safely
because they want to not because they have to; they work to eliminate hazard

because it is the right thing to do. The broad aim of this chapter is to share with you concepts and tools that will enable you to create this kind of values-based, self-governing environment.

OBJECTIVES

By the end of this chapter, you will:

- **Increase your understanding of the ingredients for creating a values-based self-governing safety culture.**
- **Assess the performance potential of your current environment.**
- **Discover tools you can use to move your culture toward a self-governing, values-based culture.**
- **Know how to use a set of tools to improve operational excellence and HSE performance.**

A REVIEW OF WORK MOTIVATION

All people pretty much need the same things – achievement, belonging, justice and fairness. All employees work so they can meet their needs. What does differ between people is their belief that they can actually meet their needs in their work environment and this, happily, is something you can influence through your leadership and coaching.

The mind is a mysterious place, but this we know about the mind - beliefs are self-fulfilling, i.e., happening or brought about as a result of being expected. If an employee thinks they can, they can; if they think they can't, they can't!!! The bottom line is that what your employees believe about their ability to meet their needs determines their level of commitment and effort.

Studies have shown that employees fall into one of three groups:

- **The disengaged**
- **The apathetic**
- **The fully engaged**

Disengaged and apathetic employees believe, with varying degrees of pessimism, that they cannot meet their needs at work. Engaged employees, on the other hand, are optimistically certain they can meet their needs through dedicated effort. When you look at the bottom line, the latter group produces more, have significantly fewer incidents and exhibit values-based self-governance. We are sure you agree these are very desirable outcomes.

LEADING FOR POSITIVE EXPECTATIONS: THE PSYCHOLOGY OF SELF-EFFICACY

Five things actively influence the degree to which your employees develop positive expectations of success at meeting their needs (see Figure 7.1). The first is the degree to which they believe they know how to be successful, that they have the skills, tools and opportunities to succeed (self-efficacy). The second is the degree to which they believe they are in control of the important outcomes available at work (response efficacy). This is the belief that I have the power and authority to do the right thing, right, even if it means stopping work in order to remove a risk. The third is the degree to which they feel optimistic (outcome-expectancy). This is the belief that their efforts will lead to the desired outcome, e.g., increased safety, reduced risk, etc. The fourth is the degree to which they believe they are valued by you and the organization. This is the belief they are important and are respected. This belief leads to the development of self-esteem. The fifth is the degree to which they believe they belong, that they are a member of the work community.

When these five beliefs are all aligned, the effect is high levels of commitment and voluntary effort on behalf of the organization. Figure 7.1 illustrates how these five states work together to influence the level of commitment and effort, which is often referred to as engagement.

Figure 7.1: Five Psychological States that Increase Engagement

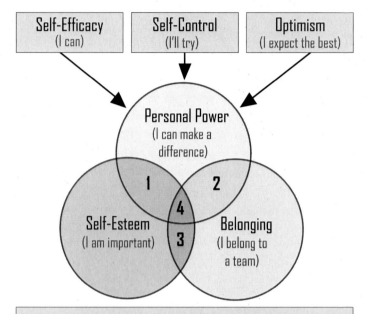

1. I can make a difference.
2. Together, we can make a difference.
3. I am a valuable team member.
4. We are important and can make a valued difference.

THE INGREDIENTS OF HIGH PERFORMANCE

The discussion so far has dealt with what each of your employees needs and with the fact that when they believe they can meet these needs at work, extraordinary things happen, like total engagement in the work. Figure 7.2 shows how the environment interacts with employees to make it more or less likely they can meet their needs. As you can see, when the organization provides opportunity, information, recognition and caring, high performance is the result (see Figure 7.2). This is not speculation by the way. This is fact!!

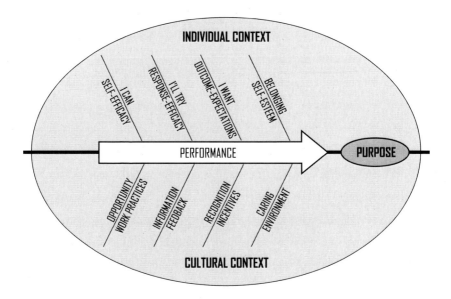

PRACTICES THAT PROMOTE COMMITMENT AND EFFORT

What can you do to promote increased employee commitment and effort? Below, you will find practices that have been shown (these practices have been researched and found to be effective) to do so. The practices are categorized so that you can make more effective use of them to assess yourself and to change what you are doing.

Enhancing Achievement Orientation through Providing Opportunity

The creation of high levels of engagement and effort starts with how you get your people to focus on what is important. We call this achievement oriented practices. These are the practices that you put in play to get your people to maintain a focus on the target – operational excellence and safety perfor-mance. To be most effective, you should:

- **Make sure employees have all the resources (equipment, tools, etc.) needed to do their job right.**
- **Empower employees with the authority and power to eliminate risk and improve performance as they see the opportunity to do so.**

- Break down long term goals into realistic short term objectives.
- Help employees to deal effectively with work related challenges and problems.
- Help your group attain their work goals.
- Help employees find solutions related to specific problems.
- Hold people accountable for goal achievement.
- Hold yourself accountable for goal achievement.

Enhancing Safety Performance through Providing Information: Role and Expectation Clarity

Clarity about what one is supposed to do and at what level is also a critical ingredient in influencing high levels of commitment and dedicated effort. Three kinds of clarity come into play: role clarity (what am I responsible for?), expectation clarity (what level of performance is expected of me?) and information clarity (how will I know how well I am performing?). To be most effective, you should:

- Make sure each employee's personal goals are aligned with team goals.
- Make sure every employee has a clear understanding of their roles and responsibilities.
- Make sure every employee gets enough information to do their job well.
- Make sure every employee understands the standards by which their performance is evaluated.
- Make sure you apply the performance standards fairly and consistently.
- Focus on and measure results.
- Make sure the performance standards by which performance is judged are clearly linked to the overall company business strategy.
- Make sure there is a high level of open communications in the group.

Enhancing Safety Performance through Providing Recognition and Coaching

Operational and Safety Excellence are always moving targets. In your role as leader/coach, you must help keep your group on track by paying attention to and recognizing what is working well and by paying attention to and correcting what needs to be improved. To be most effective, you should:

- **Make sure every employee receives frequent feedback about how well they are performing relative to their goals.**
- **Make sure every employee receives meaningful feedback that helps them improve their performance.**
- **Reward and recognize people in a way that matches their performance and achievements.**
- **Provide coaching and training to those whose performance needs improving.**
- **Provide ample opportunities to learn and develop new skills.**

Enhancing Safety Performance through Creating a Caring Culture

Your aim is to create a values-based self-governing culture in which people achieve the goal of No Incident/No One Gets Hurt because they do not just comply with the values and rules of the organization but are committed to them. They behave safely because this is what they want and choose to do. At this point, employees can be said to own the values of the group.

You can demonstrate caring by doing more of the following:

- **Get to know your employees.**
- **Let your employees know you.**
- **Treat each employee with respect and dignity.**
- **Seek employee opinion on how to improve safety.**
- **Act on the opinions when they have merit.**

THE VALUES-BASED SELF-GOVERNING CULTURE

Ultimately, you would like to create a values-based safety culture. What is safety culture? For our purposes, culture is the DNA of the organization, the sum total of its history, values, aspirations and endeavors.

Culture informs members about:

- **What is important (values)?**
- **What is real (open, transparent information)?**
- **What is possible (how one should behave)?**

Mastering culture is no longer a job for just those at the top of the organizational chart. An organizational culture represents the collective action of all the individuals that comprise it, so it is incumbent upon everyone who wants to do well to understand the intricacies of how culture works. Blind obedience, informed acquiescence and values-based self-governance are not just types of culture; they also describe an approach to governing. Blind obedience and informed acquiescence cultures place most governance outside the individual in the hands of a boss or a set of rules. Values-based self-governance places governance squarely on the shoulders of each person in the culture and in these cultures, each is enfranchised to act quickly and autonomously when presented with opportunities to improve performance and safety. Values-based self-governing cultures are also sustainable cultures.

Self-governance shifts decision making from the pragmatic to the principled

Values-based self-governance cultures are inspired by a mission and steered by values. They enshrine long-term principles in place of short-term gain and challenge each person to fulfill them in every act they perform. Decisions made on the basis of sound principles provide a steady rudder in stormy seas.

Self-governance is a higher concept

Values-based self-governance governs in the name of principles and values, not rules, and only principles and values have the ability to inspire. The cultures speak in the language of should rather than can. They call us forth to wed our highest goals and aspirations to how we do what we do each day. If values become the engine of culture, self-governance provides the scaffolding that allows everyone throughout the hierarchy to embrace and put into operation those values daily in everything that they do.

CREATING THE SUSTAINABLY SAFE CULTURE

Figure 7.3 summarizes how you can create and sustain a values-based self-governing work culture. Each box represents a set of decisions or the practices that flow from them. In turn, each box is an input into the next box in the chain. The lines connecting the boxes represent the flow of influence that produces or results in engagement and competent performance. The words next to each of the connecting lines represent influences that impact or moderate the flow of influence. We refer to this as the High Performance Model.

The High Performance Model illustrates the evolution of competent, committed, hard working employees. It starts with the decisions made and reinforced by senior leadership regarding employee involvement, learning and development, rewards and recognition and well-being (read Box 1).

These decisions get translated into leadership practices that empower employees, hold them to a high standard of excellence, provide recognition based on merit and protect each person's health and safety (read Box 2).

These practices reinforce achievement, the development of belonging/connectedness to the organization, performance excellence, learning and innovation and the level of commitment, effort and alignment with the values of the organization (read Box 3).

Committed, aligned, engaged employees exhibit self-governance and deliver superior performance (read Box 4).

Organizations that deliver superior performance produce superior results in the market place (read box 5).

The connecting words reflect the qualities that become characteristic of the organization over time. For example, as the organization's true values (Box 1) get incorporated into the day to day management of the organization (Box 2) and these influence employee behaviors and outcomes (Box 3), culture evolves. A quality of every culture is its climate - the prevailing set of attitudes that come to typify the organization. Another aspect of culture is work practices. These are local influences that affect the ability of employees to meet their needs at work. Finally, all of these influences take place over time. It takes time for a culture to evolve and it takes time to change one too.

Proper leadership practices aligned with a mission yield engaged, competent employees – those that use their voluntary effort to execute consistent, repeatable, effective work practices. In other words, appropriate leadership practices create self-governing employees who choose to excel because they want to.

IMPROVING YOUR COACHING

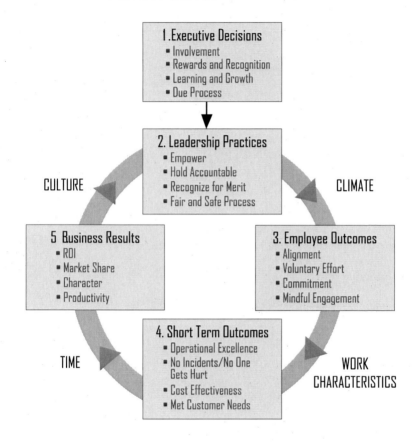

How well are you doing at creating a high performance environment?
If you want to find out, have your employees complete Tool 7.1 -
The Organizational Performance Potential Audit found on the Coaching
Resources Website and described in Chapter 9. This tool will aid in a dialogue
with your employees about how to make your workspace more receptive to
performance and safety excellence.

Chapter 8:
The Basics for Those in a Hurry

I never cease to be amazed at the power of the coaching process to draw out the skills or talent that was previously hidden within an individual, and which invariably finds a way to solve a problem previously thought unsolvable.

JOHN RUSSELL

INTRODUCTION

There are just a few core ideas in each chapter. The rest of the content is there to deepen your appreciation and understanding of these core ideas because your actions can be no wiser than your thoughts. Chapter 8 is a summary of the core ideas from each chapter.

AND NOW - THE BASIC TRUTHS AND IDEAS

Introduction

This book is based on the premise that sustainable safety is possible when a culture is values-based and self-governing. We used the acronyms COP and ACE to compared and contrast these two philosophical approaches to safety.

COP stands for control, order and prescribe. It is the basis for most behavioral based safety programs. From this stance, safety is achieved though safety systems, education and compliance to procedures and rules. The result of this stance is that safety performance is managed by forces that are extrinsic to the individual employees, and it is well known that extrinsic motivation quickly and inevitably habituates. This is the nature of extrinsic control – its effects are only temporary – and of the all too human tendency to break rules in order to find short cuts.

ACE stands for acknowledge, commit and empower. From this stance, safety is achieved not just by systems design, education and compliance, but also by commitment and internal motivation. The result of this is that employees act safely not because they have to but because they choose to; they value safety, which is to say that safety is an intrinsic desire. When people value and are committed to safety you aren't looking for violations, but for opportunities for process and safety improvement.

You create a values-based, self-governing ACE work culture by creating a relationship focus and an achievement orientation in your work group. These two abilities are the key to your success as a coach.

Chapter 1: What Coaching Is and Why You Need to Coach

Coaching is the process of creating a relationship based, learning oriented endeavor. There are several key words in this definition:

Process: coaching is not an event but a process, a well planned and executed series of steps designed to meet a learning need. The basic steps of this process are to spot a need, plan a course of action, implement it with the learner, have them reflect on their actions and acquire new knowledge, skills and attitudes.

Create: coaching doesn't just happen. You must create the process in which learning can take place. Since every situation is unique, you must constantly be co-creating the space in which learning can take place.

Relationship: the foundation of every coaching process is a relationship based on high trust and low fear. If you can't establish trust with your employees you cannot coach, period.

Learning: the aim of coaching is to enable learning. This means that coaching is very goal directed.

Endeavor: An endeavor is a conscientious and concerted effort toward an end – enabling the learning of new behavior. Coaching is never happenstance – it is well planned and executed.

Every one of us has to learn how to be successful and as a leader your role is to enable people to be successful. Not only does this involve creating a work space in which it is possible to succeed, it also means that, from time to time, you will have to teach your employees new ways of being and guide them back from the brink of failure. This is what coaching is. So, to be a great leader, you must also be a great coach.

Chapter 2: Creating the Coaching Relationship

The foundation of successful coaching is a relationship built on high trust and low fear. Such relationships can be said to grow and develop through four levels or stages:

Trusting – the foundation of safety is to build an atmosphere of trust, which, in behavioral terms is doing what you say you are going to do and treating each person with dignity and respect. Learning is possible only when high levels of trust are present. Trust grows when you are personal, keep your word and ensure the safety of every person. Trust paves the way for opening.

Opening – safety is possible only when information is available for discussion and analysis. Opening is the process of achieving transparency. The level of openness depends on the level of trust. To enable learning, you have to know the learner, you have to understand their motivations, their worries, their way of learning and their limits. High trust helps the learner feel free to share these things with you and in the sharing, you come to understand how to engage the learner in the process of realizing.

Realizing – people are naturally goal oriented. As information is shared, opportunities for process improvement and learning will become evident. Ultimately it is the learner who must learn, you are not in direct control of this; however, if you have freed the learner to be open with you, they will readily accept your coaching and they will, under most circumstances, learn and move toward inter-being or partnership.

Inter-being – as opportunities for growth and learning become evident, so do opportunities for collaboration and teamwork, which grow out of the group's shared values and goals. Your ultimate aim as a coach is to create a sustainable high performance, safe environment. This is an environment in which every employee is capable of and committed to operational excellence and safe performance. It is an environment in which employees are fully engaged in the work of the team. It is an environment of No Incident/No One Gets Hurt.

To be a successful coach you must learn how to move your work environment along the pathway of high trust and low fear. You accomplish this by:

- **Being personal and open.**
- **Getting to know your people.**
- **Engaging employees in frequent conversations.**
- **Using questions to find out who they are, what they do and why.**
- **Using "I" statements.**
- **Owning your feelings (avoid blaming others for how you feel).**
- **Being responsible for your reactions to others.**
- **Sharing only what can be handled at the time and avoiding data dumps.**
- **Being conscious of your intentions for sharing.**
- **Being sensitive to the timing of your self-disclosure.**
- **Contributing to rapport and problem solving.**
- **Listening to others.**

Chapter 3: Your Behavioral Style Influences Success

Each of us develops a unique style of being in our role as leader/coach. This style is determined by our priority (people or tasks) and by our preferred pace of working (passive or active). Priority and pace interact and lead each of us to develop one of four basic styles: Dominant, Influencing, Steady or Compliant. Your style is neither right nor wrong; however, each style has both positive and negative impacts on others, depending on their style. The challenge is for you to adapt your style to the individual you are coaching. To become more flexible, you must understand how your style impacts the way you are, the way you are seen and the way others respond to your efforts to influence them. Styles are neither wrong nor right; they just are. Still, they are not without an impact.

Your challenge is to:

Be aware of your style. You can't change what you don't understand. You can increase your awareness by completing some sort of behavioral profile (see Chapter 9). You can also increase your awareness by asking others to give you feedback. Each style has its own unique pattern of thinking, feeling and doing.

Understanding your style's impact. When you interact with others, they make judgments about your person based on what they observe. These impressions determine how receptive they will be to your coaching efforts. You can come to understand your impact by reading the feedback provided by the behavioral profile, and by observing past coaching efforts. Keep in mind that those you coach also have a style and it influences them just like your style will influence you. So, if you are a dominant style, how do you think another dominant style will respond to your coaching? The key is to understand your style so that you can achieve a sense of balance.

Adapt it to meet the requirements of the situation. You can increase or decrease your openness (task versus people preference) and/or directness (passive versus active preference) by:

· Increasing Your Openness (Increasing Your People Focus) –

helps you show/demonstrate greater interest in others.
· Decreasing Your Openness (Increasing Your Task Focus) –
helps you place greater emphasis on tasks.
· Increasing Directness (Increasing Your Pace) –
helps you accomplish more in less time.
· Decreasing Directness (Decreasing Your Pace) –
helps you slow down a bit and get in tune with your employees.

Chapter 4: The Basics of Adult Learning

Successful coaching requires that you understand why and how adults learn. This means that you understand why people learn, how they learn best and how to use this knowledge to create effective learning experiences.

Motivation and Expectations: Learning occurs when people are motivated to learn. Level of motivation, in turn, is influenced by the degree to which the learner believes their effort will produce a tangible reward. We call this belief an expectation. Expectations are self-fulfilling. People act in a way that whatever they expect to get, they get. This means you have to apply the principles of adult learning to ensure the learner develops the expectation of success.

Principles that reinforce the expectation of success:

Principle 1: Behavior operates on the environment. A person engages in a given behavior because it produces a predictable outcome (or helps them avoid a predictable outcome). Behaviors that consistently produce (or avoid) a given outcome are repeated over and over and become habits. This relationship is moderated by the person's expectations.

Principle 2: The Principle of Reinforcement. If you want a behavior to occur more or less frequently, you have to ensure that the behavior is consistently followed by an appropriate reinforcement.

Principle 3: Relevance. Adults learn best when they can clearly see the benefit of learning.

Principle 4: Repetition. Learning requires practice, so you can improve your coaching by ensuring that the learner has many opportunities for practicing the required behaviors.

Principle 5: Results. Success breeds success. Strive to arrange the coaching process so that the learner experiences frequent success.

Principle 6: Involvement. Adults learn best when they trust you, so it is important that you establish many positive involvements with the learner.

Principle 7: Doing. Adults learn best by doing rather than by rote. This means your coaching should involve the learner doing something as opposed to just observing you or stopping something.

Principle 8: Pace. Learning spread over a relatively long period of time tends to be more effective that learning crammed into a small window of time.

Principle 9: Individualize. Since each learner is more or less unique, you should strive to adapt your coaching style to the learner's style.

Principle 10: Problem Solving. Adults learn best through experience. Set up learning so that the learner has to solve a problem.

Chapter 5: STEER

Successful coaching always follows a strategy. In other words, successful coaches have a structure they use to plan and execute their coaching. The basis of the structure is that it enables the learner to plan, do, reflect and learn in a systematic manner but only if you understand how to adapt your coaching to the learning style of the learner. If you use the STEER model, this takes places as part of the structure.

We have used the word STEER to capture the key elements of this process:

S = Spot a coaching opportunity.

An opportunity arises when there is a learning need.

· Diagnose the need. Distinguish between needs stemming from problems with the WAY and those stemming from problems of the WILL.

T = Tailor your coaching to the learner's style of learning.

Each person is unique so effective coaches individualize their coaching to the requirements and challenges presented by the specific person to be coached.

E = Explain and demonstrate how to perform successfully.

Every need is a multi-leveled. It has a mental component, a behavioral component and an attitudinal component. You must explain and demonstrate each of these so that the learner can develop a mental model of what the expected behavior is and what success looks like.

E = Empower to perform successfully.

Provide the learner the tools, the resources and the plan to learn the new way of being.

R = Recognize and reinforce learning and behavior change.

Learning is a process not an event. You must provide patience, ongoing reinforcement (recognition) and support for this process to unfold fully.

Chapter 6: GUIDE

Sometimes a learning need is rooted in a poor attitude or a negative expectation. At these times, the tactic must shift from a primarily teaching mode to a behavior change mode. We refer to this process as GUIDE in order to emphasize the need to shift your thinking from that of teacher to that of counselor. In this role, your primary challenge is to help the learner choose between two pathways: one that is self-defeating and one that is self-enhancing.

The challenge is to use your relationship skills to get the learner to the point at which they can understand they have a choice, that it is their responsibility to make it and that they are accountable for doing so. The following steps will help you become more effective in doing this:

G = Get involved at a personal level. The challenge for you is to get to know the learner to such an extent that you can participate in his exploration of how he has gotten to the place he's at, one that consistently produces the discomfort and pain they experience.

U = Use questions to enable understanding of current behavior. This positive involvement builds the level of trust required for you to help the learner become aware of their current behavior and to see how their pain is a result of that behavior.

I = Help the learner to investigate natural consequences and make new choices about what they want. Once you have explored current behavior and its natural consequences you are in a position to help the learner see they have alternatives and the power to create more positive outcomes for themself.

D = Develop a learning plan. Learning new expectations takes time and structure. Here your role is to help the learner develop a get better plan, one that is under their control and that they can execute today. This is often a difficult step for the learner as they are not used to doing this or they would be doing so already. Your challenge is to help them develop a plan that:
· Is simple enough to ensure initial success.
· Is a DO plan rather than a stop doing plan.
· Is non-contingent; dependent on the learner's choices and actions and not on others.
· Is a NOW plan, something that can be started immediately.
· Is specific.
· Requires a commitment.

E = Encourage change. To increase the likelihood the learner learns, you must show them that you will be there for them. You do this by following up and never giving up; however, you also must learn to discipline yourself to allowing natural consequences to take place.

Chapter 7: The High Performance Environment

Ultimately, as a leader, your aim is to create and sustain high levels of operational excellence and safety performance. This is possible only when high levels of operational excellence and safety performance reflect the deep-seated commitments of each of your employees. It is said that your thoughts can be no wiser than your understanding and your actions no wiser than your thoughts. As a leader, you can be no more successful than your level of understanding of the ingredients in sustainable high levels of operational excellence and safety performance. So what do you need to understand and implement to create the sustainable high performance environment? Here are the basics:

Enhance Achievement Orientation through Providing Opportunity

The creation of high levels of engagement and effort starts with how you get your people to focus on what is important. We call this achievement oriented practices. These are the practices that you put in play to get your people to maintain a focus on the target – operational excellence and safety performance.

Enhancing Safety Performance through Providing Information: Role and Expectation Clarity

Clarity about what one is supposed to do and at what level is a critical ingredient in influencing high levels of commitment and dedicated effort. Three kinds of clarity come into play: 1. Role clarity (What am I responsible for?); 2. Expectation clarity (What level of performance is expected of me?); 3. Information clarity, (How will I know how well I am performing?).

Enhancing Safety Performance through Providing Recognition and Coaching

Operational and Safety Excellence are always moving targets. In your role as leader/coach, you must help keep your group on track by paying attention to and recognizing what is working well and by noticing and correcting what needs to be improved.

Enhancing Safety Performance through Creating a Caring Culture

Your aim is to create a values-based, self-governing culture in which people achieve the goal of No Incident/No One Gets Hurt because they do not just comply with the values and rules of the organization, but are committed to them. They behave safely because this is what they want and choose to do. At this point, employees can be said to own the values of the group.

Part 5: Tools for Improving Your Coaching Practices

Chapter 9:
Tools For Developing and Delivering Coaching

Don't measure yourself by what you have accomplished,
but by what you should have accomplished with your ability.

Success comes from knowing that you did your best to become
the best that you are capable of becoming.

JOHN WOODEN

BACKGROUND

Every effective coach has an array of resources and tools at their disposal.
The tools are the backbone of every coach's practice, the means by which the
coach thinks through the process, what they hope to accomplish, the steps
required and the resources needed to ensure success.

OBJECTIVES

By the end of this chapter, you will be able to:

- **Use a number of resources to increase awareness
  of your coaching practices.**
- **Select and use tools that will improve your ability
  to deliver effective coaching.**
- **Become more adept at creating your own personal coaching tools.**

RESOURCES FOR IMPROVING YOUR COACHING PRACTICE

There are many ways to improve your coaching practice. You could attend a workshop, for example, which gives you an opportunity to practice your skills and get feedback at the same time. However, if you are like the authors, time is often in short supply. In this unique resource section, we share a set of tools that we have found to be useful in helping us improve our own coaching practice. These tools are described below and they are available on-line. To access the tools on-line, go to our web sites and click on the Coaching Resources Icon or visit www.coaching-dna.com.

The following breakdown provides a brief description of each of the coaching tools as well as the way to use the tool as you develop your coaching practices. The tools are organized by chapter so that you can easily see what it intended to help you accomplish. For example, since your beliefs are critical in determining why and how you approach the task of coaching, Chapter 1 introduces you to the Core Beliefs Inventory. This tool allows you to examine and reflect on the core beliefs you bring to your coaching practice.

Tools for Improving Your Coaching Practices

9-1: What Coaching Is and Why You Need to Coach

Tool 1.1 - Core Beliefs Inventory

This tool is a self-assessment and provides you insight into your core beliefs about human nature. Since beliefs shape perception and tend to be self-fulfilling, the Core Beliefs Inventory can increase your awareness of the impact these beliefs have on your coaching practice.

Tool 1.2 - Coaching Skills Assessment

This tool can be used as a self-assessment or as a 360 degree assessment of skills associated with effective coaching. The feedback from this tool can be used to assess your own learning needs and guide the development of a plan to improve these skills. An output from this assessment is a library of learning modules to help you improve in those areas where the feedback indicates.

9-2: Creating a Coaching Relationship

Tool 2.1 - TORI Assessment

TORI is an acronym for the stages in the development of every relationship, including coaching relationships. This self-assessment helps you become aware of how you approach relationships and also provides insight into how you may behave at cross-purposes with the development of relationships that foster learning and collaboration.

Tool 2.2 - Effective Coaching Relationships

Learning and change don't just happen – they require nurturing in an environment in which there is a high level of trust and feedback. This tool helps you discover the effectiveness of your coaching relationships.

9-3: Behavioral Style and Your Coaching Effectiveness

Tool 3.1: Behavioral Style Evaluation

This self-assessment identifies your typical style of interacting with others: DOMINANT, INFLUENCING, STEADY, CONVENTIONAL. There is no right or wrong style and every style has both positives and negatives. This tool helps you appreciate these positive and negative aspects in yourself and others. The aim is to be able to adapt your style to the requirements of the situation. The tool also provides insights into how you can increase your behavioral flexibility.

9-4: The Basics of Adult Learning and Motivation

Tool 4.1: Assumptions About Learners and Learning

Everybody learns differently. Some people learn best by listening and thinking while others learn best through hands-on experiences. To maximize your coaching effectiveness, you must understand the learner's style and then adapt your coaching to that style.

9-5: Handling Problems of the Way: The STEER Model

Tool 5.1: Spotting Coaching Opportunities

This activity is useful in helping you spot and prioritize the many coaching opportunities you are likely to encounter on a day to day basis.

Tool 5.2: Diagnosing a Need

To deliver effective coaching, you must be able to discriminate needs that are caused by a lack of knowledge and skill versus those that are caused by a negative attitude. This activity helps you distinguish between the two kinds of needs and select a strategy that is most appropriate to the specific need.

Tool 5.3: Developing a Coaching Plan

Effective coaching is disciplined and follows a process that includes spotting coaching opportunities, diagnosing and analyzing a need, developing a coaching plan, delivering coaching and following up. In this section, you will find a collection of worksheets to help you accomplish each of these tasks.

Tool 5.4: Delivering Coaching

This tool is actually a set of checklists that define each step in the STEER model in behavioral terms. You can use these lists to evaluate your coaching after the fact and find out if you are leaving out important elements of the coaching process. This feedback can assist you as you strive to become a more effective coach.

9-6: Handling Problems of the Will: The GUIDE Model

Tool 6.1: Attitude Problems that Need Resolving

This tools helps you sort through those pesky problems you are likely to encounter at work and determine their origin: a lack of skill or a poor attitude.

Tool 6.2: Diagnosing a Need

To deliver effective coaching, you must be able to discriminate needs that are caused by a lack of knowledge and skill versus those that are caused by a negative attitude. This activity helps you distinguish between the two kinds of needs and selects a strategy that is most appropriate to the specific need.

Tool 6.3: The Counseling Skills Checklist

This tool provides an opportunity for you to evaluate and enhance your skills and effectiveness dealing with problems that arise from a lack of motivation. These problems are referred to as problems involving the WILL and are often found in people who have the skills to be successful but who aren't successful.

Tool 6.4: Developing the Get Better Plan

To work, a get better plan requires committed effort on the part of the learner. This tool shows you how to develop a plan that works in helping the learner develop the responsibility and discipline they will need to change their attitude.

Tool 6.5: Delivering Counseling

A series of checklists you can use to perform an evaluation of your counseling skill or have an independent observer do so.

9-7: The High Achievement Environment

Tool 7.1 - The Organizational Performance Potential Audit

Wherever they are found, High Achievement Environments have a number of things in common. The Organizational Performance Potential Audit is a team assessment by which the members of your work group evaluate their work environment. The feedback can be used to identify gaps in this environment that can then be targeted for improvement.

Tool 7.2: Designing Empowering Jobs

This activity will help you design jobs that empower each of your direct reports to achieve high levels of operational and safety performance.

9-8: Tools for Those in a Hurry

Tool 8.1: Personal Planning Contract Form

As you work through this book, you will inevitably discover areas in which you need to develop your knowledge, skills and attitudes. This form will serve as your guide for doing so. It can also be used as a basis for seeking your own coaching.

9-1: What Coaching Is and Why You Need to Coach

Tool 1.1: The Core Beliefs Inventory

Purpose

Coaching effectiveness is built on a foundation comprised of:

- Your values, which organize your personality, including how you think and problem solve
- Your skills
- Your job knowledge (see Figure 9.1)

FIGURE 9.1: Pillars of COACHING EFFECTIVENESS

EFFECTIVE COACHING

SKILLS   VALUES   KNOWLEDGE

Of these three pillars, your values are perhaps the most important. You can have all the skills and job knowledge in the world, but that won't make you an effective coach if your values are inconsistent with the role of coach. Ultimately, what you do when faced with a coaching opportunity is determined by your values.

All behavior is a reflection of a person's values. Your true values are reflected in the actions you take. In fact, this is how value is defined. A value guides action. Values are reflected in our beliefs about what is and isn't worthwhile. If you want to know what your values are, observe your behaviors. Every action reflects a set of choices that you make...

- **To be aware of the choice or to deny it.**
- **To be aware of alternatives or to be locked into only one option.**
- **To take action or not to take action.**
- **To do this and rather than that.**

This book introduces many new skills. To apply these skills in the best possible way, it is important that you examine the values revealed in your behavior, and that you strive to develop and enhance those values that will enable you to learn. To become the most effective coach possible, you need to approach the experience of learning in the same way that those whom you coach must approach the experience of learning - with openness, receptivity to change and a willingness to work hard to create change. The goals of this activity are to help you:

- **Develop awareness of your most important values.**
- **Understand the gaps between what you say you value and what you really value.**
- **Position yourself to begin working through and eliminating those gaps.**
- **Become aware of when you are and are not producing desired outcomes or results.**

Directions

The Core Beliefs Inventory consists of thirty-two pairs of statements. Choose and circle which statement within each pair is most typical of you in most situations, most of the time.

1.	H	During my spare time, I have no trouble finding things to do.
	P	During my spare time, I often have trouble finding things to do.
2.	S	I feel very sure of myself.
	D	I am usually unsure of myself.
3.	T	My managers/supervisors have, for the most part, been very helpful.
	M	My managers/supervisors have, for the most part, shown a lack of understanding.
4.	O	I allow my feelings to show.
	C	I don't allow my feelings to show.
5.	H	I have been very lucky so far.
	P	Luck has not played a role in getting me where I am.
6.	D	I am sometimes overcome by feelings of loneliness and worthlessness.
	S	I generally feel comfortable, even when I am alone.
7.	M	I doubt the honesty of people who are more friendly than they have to be.
	T	Just because people are friendly doesn't mean they are dishonest.
8.	O	I frequently expose myself to new learning opportunities.
	C	I find there is little time to learn new things.
9.	H	I am generally happy.
	P	I am generally unhappy.
10.	D	My friends don't need me as much as I need them.
	S	My friends need me just as much as I need them.
11.	T	Most people will admit their mistakes, even when it would be just as easy to blame someone.
	M	Most people try to blame someone else to cover up for their own mistakes.
12.	O	It is easy for me to listen to feedback without becoming defensive.
	C	I find I often become defensive when I listen to feedback.
13.	H	I get a great deal of fun out of my life.
	P	I rarely seem to find life much fun.
14.	S	When someone thinks badly of me, this is of no great cause for concern.
	D	When someone thinks badly of me, I worry about it.
15.	M	It is mainly fear of being caught that keeps people honest.
	T	People are basically honest.
16.	C	I find it very hard to deal with conflicts.
	O	I find it quite easy to deal with conflicts.
17.	H	Most problems can be solved if one takes action.

	P	It often doesn't do any good to even try to solve problems.
18.	S	When criticized wrongly for something I did not do, I do not feel guilty.
	D	When criticized wrongly for something I did not do, I still feel a bit guilty.
19.	T	Most people are nice.
	M	Most people are objectionable and have hidden motives.
20.	C	If I disagree with another person, I tend to keep quiet.
	D	If I disagree with another person, I tend to let that person know.
21.	H	Things generally work out for the best.
	P	Things just naturally have a way of going sour.
22.	S	I sleep well at night, no matter what.
	D	I often have trouble sleeping at night.
23.	T	I am very critical of other people's work.
	M	I am generally very accepting of other people's work.
24.	D	I readily share my personal views on just about everything.
	C	I am very selective with whom I share my personal views on certain topics.
25.	H	During ordinary difficulties, I generally keep up hope.
	P	It is hard for me to keep up hope, even during ordinary difficulties.
26.	S	When one small thing after another goes wrong, I go on as usual.
	D	When one small thing after another goes wrong, I feel overcome.
27.	T	People generally do what they say they are going to do.
	M	You generally have to check up on others because they rarely do what they say they are going to do.
28.	C	I feel very uncomfortable telling others what I like about them.
	D	I feel very comfortable telling others what I like about them.
29.	H	Generally, I am a person of great faith.
	P	Generally, I am a person of little faith.
30.	D	I often feel guilty about even small mistakes.
	S	I rarely feel guilty, even when I make mistakes.
31.	T	Most people are inclined to look out for others.
	M	Most people just look out for themselves.
32.	D	My friends say that I am easy to get to know.
	C	My friends say that I am hard to get to know.

Scoring and Interpretation

Count the number of H's and P's you circled and record the number in the blanks below. The total of H + P should equal eight. Likewise, total the number of S's and D's you circled, the number of T's and M's, and the number of A's and C's. Subtract the number of P's from the number of H's; the number of D's from the number of S's; the number of M's from the number of T's; and the number of C's from the number of O's. The differences can range from +8 to -8. Transfer the difference scores to the scoring profile when you are done.

H: _____ - P: _____ = _____

S: _____ - D: _____ = _____

T: _____ - M: _____ = _____

O: _____ - C: _____ = _____

																		SCORING PROFILE
Pessimism	-8	-7	-6	-5	-4	-3	-2	-1	0	1	2	3	4	5	6	7	8	Hope
Doubt	-8	-7	-6	-5	-4	-3	-2	-1	0	1	2	3	4	5	6	7	8	Confidence
Mistrust	-8	-7	-6	-5	-4	-3	-2	-1	0	1	2	3	4	5	6	7	8	Trust
Closed	-8	-7	-6	-5	-4	-3	-2	-1	0	1	2	3	4	5	6	7	8	Open

INTERPRETATION

Hope. This scale measures the degree to which you expect the best from life. Research tells us that those who expect the best from themselves and others more often obtain the best than do those who are pessimistic. The most effective coaches tend to be very hopeful. To increase your sense of hope you could:

- Comment on the positive parts of a plan or an idea before suggesting problems or revisions.
- Attend funny movies and "belly laugh." See something funny in normal everyday situations.
- Watch your speech pattern. Say "choose to" or "am going to" instead of "I have to."

Self-Confidence. This scale measures the degree to which you believe that you can, by your own efforts, influence future events, that you will do well in what you try and that you feel as smart and as capable as others. Effective coaches tend to be self-confident as opposed to being full of self-doubt. To increase your sense of confidence you could:

Decide if a given task is one you want to do well or merely complete to a satisfactory level.
  · Make a list of your strengths and skills. Keep it up to date.
    Use it as a check list when someone gives you "constructive criticism" concerning your "faults."

Trust. This scale measures the degree to which you trust others and have confidence in their good intentions. Effective coaches are essentially trusting. This belief in others acts as a self-fulfilling prophecy. To increase your sense of trust you could:
  · Take what people say at face value. Believe that what people say is what they mean. Do not look for hidden messages and motives.
  · Put in sanctions or natural consequences when making agreements. Do not use punishment after the fact. If agreements are not kept, let the natural consequences follow, but do not add punishment.

Openness. This scale measures the degree to which you are willing to self-disclose to the world. The most effective coaches are willing to share, as well as to listen. To increase your sense of openness you could:
  · Start each day by deciding to learn something new.
  · Express what you are thinking and feeling at the time of an event or conversation.

Reflection

1. What are your core beliefs?

2. What do your scores suggest about you and your view of the world?

3. What effect do these beliefs have on you and on your ability to coach others?

Tool 1.2: The Coaching Skills Assessment

The Person I am Rating is: _____ (Name)

Check one: ☐ Self Rating   ☐ Other Rating

Purpose

The Coaching Skills Assessment has been created to assist the participant in assessing their current level of competency as a coach. The rating is based on a number of behavioral competencies which are components of the coaching role. The role of coach is important in teaching the skills, stimulating the desires and encouraging the beliefs that will enable a person to succeed. Coaching refers to the set of skills required to enable high performance. The coach provides a climate of support in which learning and growth may take place.

Directions

1. Rate how effective you perceive this person to be at each skill in the checklist using the effectiveness scale described below.

If you have never observed this person performing this skill respond 0 – "Don't Know".

1	2	3	4	5	6	7
Very Ineffective	Ineffective	Somewhat Ineffective	Neither Effective nor Ineffective	Somewhat Effective	Effective	Very Effective

Darken the number which best describes your opinion on the set of numbers to the left of each statement

Example

⓪ ① ② ③ ④ ❺ ⑥ ⑦   4. Identifies and solves problems as soon as possible.

2. Next, at the end of each Dimension there is space provided for you to respond to what you think this person should STOP, START or CONTINUE doing in this area to be more effective.

Dimension 1: Developing a High Performance Environment – Individual and Team

⓪①②③④⑤⑥⑦	1. Facilitates the definition and development of team and department goals.
⓪①②③④⑤⑥⑦	2. Helps establish mutually agreed on performance goals for each person.
⓪①②③④⑤⑥⑦	3. Ensures that feedback about performance is readily available to you and to others.
⓪①②③④⑤⑥⑦	4. Ensures that the resources needed to succeed are available.
⓪①②③④⑤⑥⑦	5. Helps each team member obtain the skills required to succeed.
⓪①②③④⑤⑥⑦	6. Ensures that performance is regularly evaluated against expectations.
⓪①②③④⑤⑥⑦	7. Makes ongoing performance feedback available to all associates.
⓪①②③④⑤⑥⑦	8. Identifies and solves problems as soon as possible.
⓪①②③④⑤⑥⑦	9. Guarantees that each team member has the data and the information required to succeed.
⓪①②③④⑤⑥⑦	10. Provides associates with positive reinforcement to encourage them to perform to their potential.
⓪①②③④⑤⑥⑦	11. Recognizes and values excellent performance.
⓪①②③④⑤⑥⑦	12. Encourages experimenting with new ways of doing things.
⓪①②③④⑤⑥⑦	13. Promotes excellence in an ongoing way.
⓪①②③④⑤⑥⑦	14. Promotes teamwork and cooperation.
⓪①②③④⑤⑥⑦	15. Works with the team to meet deadlines and solve problems.
⓪①②③④⑤⑥⑦	16. Seeks to understand and address team concerns, issues and problems.

What should this person START/STOP/CONTINUE doing?

Dimension 2: Creating a Climate of Trust and Risk Taking

⓪①②③④⑤⑥⑦	17. Shares openly with associates.
⓪①②③④⑤⑥⑦	18. Spends time with associates on a regular basis.

Dimension 2: Creating a Climate of Trust and Risk Taking

⓪①②③④⑤⑥⑦	19. Listens to associates views about the job and the organization.
⓪①②③④⑤⑥⑦	20. Keeps commitments.
⓪①②③④⑤⑥⑦	21. Develops trust between associates and self.
⓪①②③④⑤⑥⑦	22. Communicates acceptance of associates.
⓪①②③④⑤⑥⑦	23. Is consistent in what he/she says and does.
⓪①②③④⑤⑥⑦	24. Is fair, open and consistent with others (i.e., shows no favoritism).
⓪①②③④⑤⑥⑦	25. Acts as a positive role model for team members.
⓪①②③④⑤⑥⑦	26. Demonstrates principles and values I admire.

What should this person START/STOP/CONTINUE doing?

COACHING SKILLS ASSESSMENT

Dimension 3: General Personnel Development

⓪①②③④⑤⑥⑦	27. Is an effective mentor and teacher.
⓪①②③④⑤⑥⑦	28. Gives fair and timely performance appraisals.
⓪①②③④⑤⑥⑦	29. Provides opportunities for team members to expand their skill and experience.
⓪①②③④⑤⑥⑦	30. Seeks to facilitate the professional development of team members.
⓪①②③④⑤⑥⑦	31. Assists team members in understanding and fulfilling their potential.
⓪①②③④⑤⑥⑦	32. Provides informal feedback during the course of a project or engagement.

What should this person START/STOP/CONTINUE doing?

Dimension 4: Valuing Individual Differences

⓪①②③④⑤⑥⑦	33. Is sensitive to balancing work and personal priorities.
⓪①②③④⑤⑥⑦	34. Listens to my ideas/views.
⓪①②③④⑤⑥⑦	35. When possible. assigns tasks well in advance of deadlines.
⓪①②③④⑤⑥⑦	36. Assigns challenging and reasonable workloads.
⓪①②③④⑤⑥⑦	37. Encourages team members to determine the best methods for accomplishing tasks.
⓪①②③④⑤⑥⑦	38. Recognizes and shows appreciation for positive contributions of team members.
⓪①②③④⑤⑥⑦	39. Seeks to fully understand contrary views before stating an opinion.

What should this person START/STOP/CONTINUE doing?

Dimension 5: Designing a Supportive Learning Environment

⓪①②③④⑤⑥⑦	40. Understands the process of skill acquisition and learning.
⓪①②③④⑤⑥⑦	41. Ensures understanding of the tasks to be performed.
⓪①②③④⑤⑥⑦	42. Jointly establishes goals for the learning process.
⓪①②③④⑤⑥⑦	43. Designs learning activities appropriate to the required performance.
⓪①②③④⑤⑥⑦	44. Clearly describes tasks to be performed and results expected from each task as needed.
⓪①②③④⑤⑥⑦	45. Clearly shows each associate how each job or role fits into the larger team or organizational context.
⓪①②③④⑤⑥⑦	46. Demonstrates or models the correct manner for performing tasks as needed.
⓪①②③④⑤⑥⑦	47. Provides consistent feedback about needed adjustments so that performance produces desired results.

What should this person START/STOP/CONTINUE doing?

COACHING SKILLS ASSESSMENT

Dimension 6: Performance Improvement Planning and Review

Scale	Item
⓪①②③④⑤⑥⑦	48. Participates with associates in jointly developing action plans.
⓪①②③④⑤⑥⑦	49. Ensures that a method for monitoring success is built into their plans.
⓪①②③④⑤⑥⑦	50. Ensures that time lines for important accomplishments are part of the plans.
⓪①②③④⑤⑥⑦	51. Acquires mutual agreement about performance improvement plans.
⓪①②③④⑤⑥⑦	52. Follows up on the plan at agreed upon times.
⓪①②③④⑤⑥⑦	53. Jointly reviews agreed upon results.
⓪①②③④⑤⑥⑦	54. Keeps commitments to follow up on their plans.

What should this person START/STOP/CONTINUE doing?

COACHING SKILLS ASSESSMENT

Dimension 7: Evaluating Performance: Giving and Receiving Feedback

Scale	Item
⓪①②③④⑤⑥⑦	55. Gets associates involved in assessing their own performance.
⓪①②③④⑤⑥⑦	56. Encourages associates to raise and discuss feelings openly.
⓪①②③④⑤⑥⑦	57. Encourages associates to describe what they are doing on the job.
⓪①②③④⑤⑥⑦	58. Helps associates identify the results of their behaviors.
⓪①②③④⑤⑥⑦	59. Helps associates examine the reasons for performance gaps.
⓪①②③④⑤⑥⑦	60. Targets feedback on behaviors that can be changed.
⓪①②③④⑤⑥⑦	61. Helps associates examine alternative ways of behaving.
⓪①②③④⑤⑥⑦	62. Uses employee input from all levels to solve problems.
⓪①②③④⑤⑥⑦	63. Listens to and encourages my ideas.
⓪①②③④⑤⑥⑦	64. Encourages open and honest communication.

(0)(1)(2)(3)(4)(5)(6)(7)	65. Clearly communicates expectations.
(0)(1)(2)(3)(4)(5)(6)(7)	66. Shares important information accurately and quickly; up, down and across the team.

What should this person START/STOP/CONTINUE doing?

(0)(1)(2)(3)(4)(5)(6)(7)	67. Finds out if associates have the resources needed to succeed.
(0)(1)(2)(3)(4)(5)(6)(7)	68. Works with associates to identify the consequences of excellent and poor performance.
(0)(1)(2)(3)(4)(5)(6)(7)	69. Discusses the consequences of various results openly.
(0)(1)(2)(3)(4)(5)(6)(7)	70. Engages associates in the process of creating and discovering multiple opportunities to learn and to succeed.

What should this person START/STOP/CONTINUE doing?

9-2: Creating a Coaching Relationship

Tool 2.1 - TORI Self-Assessment

Purpose

To understand your approach to relating to others at the level of your core beliefs and assumptions.

Directions

In front of each of the following items, place the letter that corresponds to your degree of agreement or disagreement with that statement.

SD = strongly disagree	D = disagree	A = agree	SA = strongly agree

	1. I feel that no matter what I might do, people generally would accept and understand me.
	2. I feel that there are large areas of me that I don't share with other people.
	3. I usually assert myself in most situations in life.
	4. I seldom seek help from others.
	5. Most people tend to trust one another.
	6. People are usually not interested in what others have to say.
	7. Most people exert little pressure on other people to try to get them to do what they should be doing.

8. Most people do their own thing with little thought for others.

9. I feel that I am usually a very cautious person.

10. I feel little need to cover up the things I do and keep them from others.

11. I usually try to do what I'm supposed to be doing.

12. I find that people are usually willing to help me when I want help or ask for it.

13. Most people in life are more interested in getting things done than in caring for each other as individuals.

14. Most people usually tell it like it is.

15. Most people do what they ought to do in life, out of a sense of responsibility to others.

16. Most people that I meet "have it together" at a fairly deep level.

17. I generally trust the people I meet.

18. I am afraid that if I showed my innermost thoughts to most people, they would be shocked.

19. In most life situations I feel free to do what I want to do.

20. I often feel that I am a minority in the groups I belong to.

21. People that I meet usually seem to know who they are; they have a real sense of being an individual.

22. Most people I know and work with are very careful to express only relevant and appropriate ideas when we do things together.

23. Most people have very clear goals and they know what they are doing in life.

24. Most groups I work with or live in have a hard time getting together and doing something they have decided to do.

25. If I left most groups I belong to, they would miss me very little.

26. I can trust most of the people I know with my most private and significant feelings and opinions.

27. I find that my goals are different from the goals of most people I work with.

28. I look forward to getting together with the people in the groups I belong to.

29. Most of the people I meet are playing roles and not being themselves.

30. Most of the people I know communicate with each other very well.

31. In most of the groups I belong to, members put pressure on each other toward group goals.

32. In an emergency, most people act in caring and effective ways.

33. I almost always feel very good about myself.

34. If I have negative feelings, I do not express them easily.

35. It is easy for me to take risks in my life.

36. I often go along with others simply because I feel a sense of obligation to do what is expected.

	37. People in the groups I belong to seem to care very much for each other as individuals.
	38. Most people tend to be dishonest.
	39. Most people I know let others be where they are and how they are.
	40. Most people prefer either to lead or to be led, rather than to work together with others as equals.
	41. My relationships with most people are impersonal.
	42. Whenever I feel strongly about something I feel comfortable expressing myself to others.
	43. I feel that I have to keep myself under wraps in most life situations.
	44. I usually enjoy working with people.
	45. Most people I know seem to play definite and clear roles and to be respected on the basis of how well they perform the roles.
	46. When the people I know have negative feelings they usually express them at some point.
	47. A large portion of the people in groups I belong to are very apathetic and passive.
	48. Most of the people I am usually with are well integrated at many levels.
	49. I feel like a unique person and I like being unique.
	50. I would feel very vulnerable telling most people I know my most secret and private feelings and opinions.
	51. Most of the people I know feel that my personal growth is important to me.
	52. I often don't feel like cooperating with others.
	53. People usually have a high opinion of my contributions to the groups I'm in and the conversations I have.
	54. Most people are afraid to be open and honest with others.
	55. The people that I know usually express what they want and put pressure on pretty well.
	56. Most people are pretty individualistic and do not work well together as members of a team.
	57. I often don't feel very good about myself as a person.
	58. I usually feel free to be exactly who I am and not to pretend I am something else.
	59. I feel that it is important in life to make a reasonable attempt to meet others' expectations of me.
	60. I feel a sense of inter connectedness with the people I associate with and would miss anyone who left my circle of friends and associates.
	61. It is easy to tell who the "in" people are in the groups I associate with.
	62. Most people listen to others with understanding and empathy.
	63. It seems to me that a great many people spend energy trying to do things they don't really want to do.
	64. I think that most people enjoy being with others.

	65. The groups that I associate with see me as an important group member.
	66. My ideas and opinions are often distorted by others.
	67. My basic goals in life are similar to the basic goals of other people.
	68. People are seldom willing to give me help on the things that really matter to me.
	69. People usually listen to the things that I say.
	70. It seems to me that when they feel negative, most people keep it to themselves.
	71. The groups that I'm associated with usually have a lot of energy that gets directed into whatever the group does.
	72. You really have to have some power if you want to get anything done in life.
	73. I often don't feel very genuine and real when I'm with people.
	74. There is very little that I don't know about my close friends.
	75. If I did what I really wanted to do in life, I would be doing different things from what I am now doing.
	76. I am often aware of how other people help me in what I am trying to do in life.
	77. It seems to me that most people live in fear.
	78. The people I know are usually very spontaneous and uninhibited with each other.
	79. Most people are very unclear about what they want out of life.
	80. Most of the groups I work with or live in have good team or cooperative relationships.
	81. I care very much for the people I associate with.
	82. People often misunderstand me and how I feel.
	83. When I am with others and we reach a decision about something we want to do I am usually in complete agreement with what we have decided.
	84. I have no real sense of belonging to the groups I associate with.
	85. In the groups I belong to, people treat others as important and significant people.
	86. It is easy for me to express positive feelings, but very difficult for me to express negative feelings to others.
	87. Most of the people I know are growing and changing all the time.
	88. It seems to me that most people need a lot of controls to keep them on the right track.
	89. I often feel defensive.
	90. I keep very few secrets from my associates.
	91. It is often not okay for me to be myself in the groups I'm in.
	92. I feel a strong sense of belonging to several groups in my life.
	93. In the groups I belong to, it is easy to see who is important and who is unimportant.

94. Most people don't keep a lot of secrets from others.
95. In the groups I belong to, a lot of our energy goes into irrelevant and unimportant things.
96. It seems to me that there is very little destructive competition among the people I know and associate with.

Tori Self-Diagnosis Scale Score Sheet

INSTRUCTIONS

The TORI Self-Diagnosis Scale yields eight scores; four depicting how you see yourself in your life in terms of the four core growth processes (Trusting-Being; Opening-Showing; Realizing-Becoming; and Inter depending-Inter being), and four capturing your sense of what the people and world around you are like. Look back at the items for one of the eight scales on the instrument to see how you responded. On the Score Sheet, circle your response for each item according to whether you marked "Strongly Disagree", "Disagree", etc. Then sum the item scores for the scale. Do the same for each scale.

TRUSTING-BEING					OPENING-SHOWING					REALIZING-BECOMING					INTER DEPENDING-INTER BEING				
	Item Score					Item Score					Item Score					Item Score			
Item	SD	D	A	SA	Item	SD	D	A	SA	Item	SD	D	A	SA	Item	SD	D	A	SA
1	0	1	2	3	2	3	2	1	0	3	0	1	2	3	4	3	2	1	0
9	3	2	1	0	10	0	1	2	3	11	3	2	1	0	12	0	1	2	3
17	0	1	2	3	18	3	2	1	0	19	0	1	2	3	20	3	2	1	0
25	3	2	1	0	26	0	1	2	3	27	3	2	1	0	28	0	1	2	3
33	0	1	2	3	34	3	2	1	0	35	0	1	2	3	36	3	2	1	0
41	3	2	1	0	42	0	1	2	3	43	3	2	1	0	44	0	1	2	3
49	0	1	2	3	50	3	2	1	0	51	0	1	2	3	52	3	2	1	0
57	3	2	1	0	58	0	1	2	3	59	3	2	1	0	60	0	1	2	3
65	0	1	2	3	66	3	2	1	0	67	0	1	2	3	68	3	2	1	0
73	3	2	1	0	74	0	1	2	3	75	3	2	1	0	76	0	1	2	3
81	0	1	2	3	82	3	2	1	0	83	0	1	2	3	84	3	2	1	0
89	3	2	1	0	90	0	1	2	3	91	3	2	1	0	92	0	1	2	3

How I See Myself in Life

T		D		R		I	

TRUSTING-BEING				OPENING-SHOWING				REALIZING-BECOMING				INTER DEPENDING-INTER BEING			
	Item Score				Item Score				Item Score				Item Score		
Item	SD	D	A	SA	Item	SD	D	A	SA	Item	SD	D	A	SA	Item	SD	D	A	SA
5	0	1	2	3	6	3	2	1	0	7	0	1	2	3	8	3	2	1	0
13	3	2	1	0	14	0	1	2	3	15	3	2	1	0	16	0	1	2	3
21	0	1	2	3	22	3	2	1	0	23	0	1	2	3	24	3	2	1	0
29	3	2	1	0	30	0	1	2	3	31	3	2	1	0	32	0	1	2	3
37	0	1	2	3	38	3	2	1	0	39	0	1	2	3	40	3	2	1	0
45	3	2	1	0	46	0	1	2	3	47	3	2	1	0	48	0	1	2	3
53	0	1	2	3	54	3	2	1	0	55	0	1	2	3	56	3	2	1	0
61	3	2	1	0	62	0	1	2	3	63	3	2	1	0	64	0	1	2	3
69	0	1	2	3	70	3	2	1	0	71	0	1	2	3	72	3	2	1	0
77	3	2	1	0	78	0	1	2	3	79	3	2	1	0	80	0	1	2	3
85	0	1	2	3	86	3	2	1	0	87	0	1	2	3	88	3	2	1	0
93	3	2	1	0	94	0	1	2	3	95	3	2	1	0	96	0	1	2	3

How I See the People World

T		D		R		I	

Interpretation Sheet

TRUSTING-BEING:

A person who scores high on this set of items is saying:

View of Myself: "I trust myself, have a fairly well-formed sense of my own being and uniqueness and feel good about myself as a person."

View of People: "I tend to see people as trusting and as providing a good environment for me to live and be in."

A *person who scores low on this set of items is saying:*

View of Myself: "I feel less trusting of myself, have a less formed sense of my own being and uniqueness and feel less well about myself as a person."

View of People: "I tend to see people as un-trusting, as impersonal and in role and as providing a somewhat threatening and defense-producing environment for me and for others."

OPENING-SHOWING:

A person who scores high on this set of items is saying:

View of Myself: "I feel free to show myself to others, show who I am and express my feelings and attitudes with little pretense or cover-up."

View of People: "I tend to see people as open and spontaneous and as willing to show themselves to each other."

A person who scores low on this set of items is saying:

View of Myself: "I feel unable to be open, vulnerable and unsafe. I think it is necessary to keep large areas of myself private and unshared."

View of People: "I tend to see people as fearful, cautious and unwilling to show feelings and opinions, particularly those feelings and opinions that are negative or non-supportive."

REALIZING-BECOMING:

A person who scores high on this set of items is saying:

View of Myself: "I feel free to take risks, assert myself, do anything that I really want to do and follow my intrinsic motivations. I have a sense of self-realization."

View of People: "I tend to see people as allowing other's their freedom and as providing an environment for me and others that nourishes our striving for intrinsic goals. People allow others to be who they are."

A person who scores low on this set of items is saying:

View of Myself: "I am aware of the pressure of extrinsic motivations. I feel that I must try to do what I am supposed to do and that I must attempt to meet the expectations of others."

View of People: "I tend to see other people as exerting pressures on me and others to conform, to do things that we may not want to do and to work towards goals that are not significant to me as a person."

INTER DEPENDING-INTER BEING:

A person who scores high on this set of items is saying:

View of Myself: "I have a strong sense of belonging to the groups that are important to me, and I enjoy working, helping or meeting with other people."

View of People: "I tend to see other people as cooperative, effective and relatively well integrated into the life around them and the groups they belong to."

A person who scores low on this set of items is saying:

View of Myself: "I do not have a strong sense of belonging to the groups of which I am a member, and do not especially enjoy working with others as a team. I have competitive, dependent feelings that get in the way of my teaming with others."

View of People: "I tend to see other people as not being cooperative and not working well with others. I see people in general as not easy to work with or team with and as having feelings that get in their way."

Tool 2.2 – Effective Coaching Relationships

Purpose

This discovery exercise helps you examine the effectiveness of your current work relationships.

Directions

Place an "N" on the scale to represent where you believe the team is NOW and an "F" on the scale to represent the desired FUTURE status of the team. Have team members complete this scale also. When you have completed your ratings, discuss them openly and ask team members to contribute ideas about how to improve the quality of the work relationships within the team.

	Very Low				Mod- erate				Very High
1. The level of trust in the work team is:	1	2	3	4	5	6	7	8	9
2. The level of positive regard and respect for each individual is:	1	2	3	4	5	6	7	8	9
3. The level of openness (sharing of useful information) is:	1	2	3	4	5	6	7	8	9
4. The extent to which opportunities for information exchange and feedback are present is:	1	2	3	4	5	6	7	8	9
5. The ability and readiness to identify and solve problems is:	1	2	3	4	5	6	7	8	9
6. The level of opportunity for individual and team achievement is:	1	2	3	4	5	6	7	8	9
7. The extent to which resources, including appropriate tools such as computers, are available is:	1	2	3	4	5	6	7	8	9
8. The degree to which incentives for individual and team achievement are available is:	1	2	3	4	5	6	7	8	9

9-3: Behavioral Style and Your Coaching Effectiveness

Tool 3.1 – Behavioral Style Evaluation

Directions

Think of five people who know you in your capacity as a leader/coach who would be willing to devote ten minutes to completing an evaluation of your behavior. Alternatively, you may choose people in your personal life. Either way, all five should come from one or the other – your professional life or your personal life.

Write your name on each of the Behavioral Style Evaluation forms and on the Behavioral Style Grid. Make five copies of the "Behavioral Style Evaluation: Other" form and give one to each person and arrange to have it returned to you in a reasonable time. In the meantime, complete the "Behavioral Style Evaluation: Self" form – be candid – and score it according to the instructions provided.

WHAT IS IT?

The Behavioral Style Evaluation is a selected list of statements and adjectives, derived from the managerial and psychological literature, that describe observable behaviors.

HOW DOES IT WORK?

First, complete the "Behavioral Style Evaluation: Self" form and plot your responses on a grid. The results profile is a behavioral self-portrait.

Then you take the five people you have selected and plot their scores on a grid. This is an 'other' portrait of your behavioral style.

HOW CAN IT HELP ME?

The self-portrait allows you to compare how you perceive your behavioral style with how others perceive it. This imparts knowledge about how you are viewed and if it is the way you see yourself. It will also help you to understand your behavioral style and increase the flexibility of your style.

Behavioral Style Evaluation: Self

Name: Date:

This is an informal survey, designed to determine how you usually interact with others in every day situations. The purpose of the questionnaire is to get a clear description of how you see yourself, so please be as candid as possible.

Compare each set of statements. Then, circle the letter S (self-contained/assessing), O (open/accepting), I (indirect) or D (direct) to the left of the statement that best describes you most of the time, in most situations and with most people. Please make a choice for each set of statements.

1.	O	Easy to get to know personally in business or unfamiliar social environments.	10.	S	Shows less enthusiasm than the average person.
	S	More difficult to get to know personally in business or unfamiliar social environments		O	Shows more enthusiasm that the average person.
2.	S	Focuses conversation on issues and tasks at hand; stays on subject.	11.	D	More likely to introduce self to others at social gatherings.
	O	Conversation reflects personal life experiences; may stray from business at hand.		I	More likely to wait for others to introduce themselves at social gatherings.
3.	I	Infrequent contributor to group conversations.	12.	O	Flexible about how own time is used by others.

	D	Frequent contributor to group conversations.		S	Disciplined about how own time is used by others.
4.	I	Tends to adhere to the Letter of the Law.	13.	S	Goes with own agenda.
	D	Tends to interpret the Spirit of the Law.		D	Goes with the flow.
5.	S	Makes most decisions based on goals, facts or evidence.	14.	D	More naturally assertive behavior.
	D	Makes most decisions based on feelings, experiences or relationships.		I	More naturally reserved behavior.
6.	I	Infrequent use of gestures and voice intonation to emphasize points.	15.	D	Tends to express own views more readily.
	D	Frequently uses gestures and voice intonation to emphasize points.		I	Tends to reserve the expression of own opinions.
7.	D	More likely to make emphatic statements like "This is so!"; "I feel ..."	16.	D	Tends to naturally decide more quickly or spontaneously.
	I	More likely to make qualified statements like "According to my sources ..."		I	Tends to naturally decide more slowly or deliberately.
8.	D	Greater natural tendency toward animated facial expressions or observable body responses during speaking and listening.	17.	S	Prefers to work independently or dictate the relationship conditions.
	S	More limited facial expressions or observable body responses during speaking and listening.		D	Prefers to work with others or be included in relationships.
9.	S	Tends to keep important personal feelings private; tends to share only when necessary.	18.	I	Naturally approaches risk or change more slowly or cautiously.
	D	Tends to be more willing to show or share feelings more freely.		D	Naturally approaches risk or change more quickly or spontaneously.

Total Number of circled:

S's =   O's =   I's =   D's =

Behavioral Style Evaluation: Other

Name: Date:

This is an informal survey to determine how the above named person usually interacts with others in everyday situations. The purpose of the questionnaire is to get a clear description of how you see this person, so please be as candid as possible.

Compare each set of statements. Then, circle the letter S (self-contained/assessing), O (open/accepting), I (indirect), or D (direct) to the left of the statement that best describes the above person most of the time, in most situations, and with most people. Please make a choice for each set of statements.

No.	Letter	Statement	No.	Letter	Statement
1.	O	Easy to get to know personally in business or unfamiliar social environments.	10.	S	Shows less enthusiasm than the average person.
	S	More difficult to get to know personally in business or unfamiliar social environments		O	Shows more enthusiasm that the average person.
2.	S	Focuses conversation on issues and tasks at hand; stays on subject.	11.	D	More likely to introduce self to others at social gatherings.
	O	Conversation reflects personal life experiences; may stray from business at hand.		I	More likely to wait for others to introduce themselves at social gatherings.
3.	I	Infrequent contributor to group conversations.	12.	O	Flexible about how own time is used by others.
	D	Frequent contributor to group conversations.		S	Disciplined about how own time is used by others.
4.	I	Tends to adhere to the Letter of the Law.	13.	S	Goes with own agenda.
	D	Tends to interpret the Spirit of the Law.		O	Goes with the flow.
5.	S	Makes most decisions based on goals, facts or evidence.	14.	D	More naturally assertive behavior.
	O	Makes most decisions based on feelings, experiences or relationships.		I	More naturally reserved behavior.
6.	I	Infrequent use of gestures and voice intonation to emphasize points.	15.	D	Tends to express own views more readily.
	D	Frequently uses gestures and voice intonation to emphasize points.		I	Tends to reserve the expression of own opinions.
7.	D	More likely to make emphatic statements like "This is so!"; "I feel ..."	16.	D	Tends to naturally decide more quickly or spontaneously.
	I	More likely to make qualified statements like "According to my sources ..."		I	Tends to naturally decide more slowly or deliberately.
8.	O	Greater natural tendency toward animated facial expressions or observable body responses during speaking and listening.	17.	S	Prefers to work independently or dictate the relationship conditions.
	S	More limited facial expressions or observable body responses during speaking and listening.		O	Prefers to work with others or be included in relationships.

9.	S	Tends to keep important personal feelings private; tends to share only when necessary.	18.	I	Naturally approaches risk or change more slowly or cautiously.
	D	Tends to be more willing to show or share feelings more freely.		D	Naturally approaches risk or change more quickly or spontaneously.

Total Number of circled:

S's =   O's =   I's =   D's =

Plotting Your Behavioral Style Profile: As You See Yourself

Directions

1. Count the number of S and O responses (together they should total 9). Do the same for the D and I responses.

2. Subtract the number of S responses from the number of O responses, then subtract the number of I responses from the number of D responses.

3. On the Behavioral Grid (Figure 9.2), make an √ on the vertical line at the number corresponding to the difference between your O and S totals. Then darken that horizontal line. (If your total is between +1 and +9, place your "x" on the O portion of the vertical line. If your total is between -1 and -9, place your "x" on the S portion of the vertical line (see Graph 1).

Example

3 O's   1 I's

6 S's   8 D's

3 O   8 D

-6 S   1 I

-3 S   7 D

4. On the same grid, make another √ on the horizontal line at the number corresponding to difference between the I and D totals (see Graph 2). Then

darken the vertical line. (If your total is between +1 and +9, place your √s on the D side of the horizontal line; if your total is between -1 and -9, place your √s on the I side of the horizontal line.

5. Make a check mark to designate your self-evaluation.

Plotting Your Behavioral Style Profile: As Others See You

Directions:

1. Using the same method, plot each of the five assessments on the same grid on which you plotted your self-evaluation (see Graph 3).

2. At the intersection of each set of darkened lines insert a √ to indicate "other."

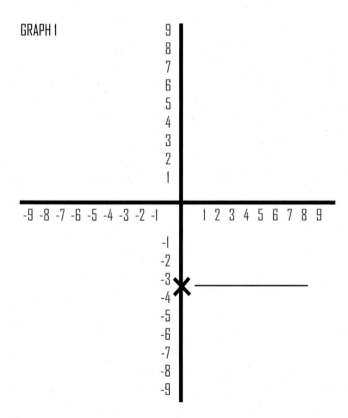

GRAPH 1

GRAPH 2

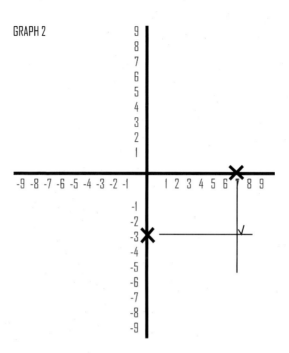

GRAPH 3

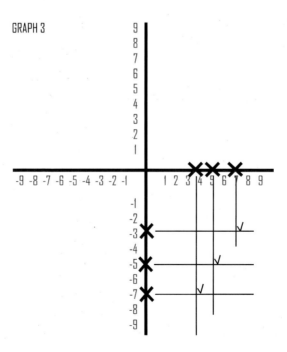

Figure 9.2 Behavioral Style Grid

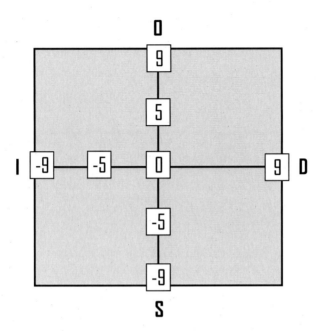

9-4: The Basics of Adult Learning and Motivation

Tool 4.1: Assumptions About Learning and Learners

Purpose

This exercise develops increased understanding of your assumptions about learning and how these assumptions affect your coaching.

Directions

Respond to each of the following statements by circling the number that most accurately explains your assumptions about learning and the learner. Use the following scale to describe your specific beliefs:

1	2	3	4	5	6	7	8	9
Never				Frequently				Always

	ASSUMPTIONS ABOUT LEARNERS AND LEARNING CHECKLIST
1 2 3 4 5 6 7 8 9	1. I believe all learners are different.
1 2 3 4 5 6 7 8 9	2. I believe that given enough time and proper instruction, learners can learn anything.
1 2 3 4 5 6 7 8 9	3. I give my learners opportunities for frequent practice.
1 2 3 4 5 6 7 8 9	4. I break instruction down into reasonable steps.

	ASSUMPTIONS ABOUT LEARNERS AND LEARNING CHECKLIST
1 2 3 4 5 6 7 8 9	5. When I coach, I give clear instructions.
1 2 3 4 5 6 7 8 9	6. The pace of learning is determined by the learner.
1 2 3 4 5 6 7 8 9	7. The learner progresses to new material when a particular step is mastered .
1 2 3 4 5 6 7 8 9	8. I carefully explain how the associate's job fits into the rest of the organization.
1 2 3 4 5 6 7 8 9	9. I provide many incentives for learning.
1 2 3 4 5 6 7 8 9	10. I influence the learning environment.
1 2 3 4 5 6 7 8 9	11. I make the learning experience enjoyable.
1 2 3 4 5 6 7 8 9	12. I get to know the learner.
1 2 3 4 5 6 7 8 9	13. I enjoy coaching.
1 2 3 4 5 6 7 8 9	14. I enjoy people.
1 2 3 4 5 6 7 8 9	15. I believe people like to learn.

The ideal response for each of these statements would have been a "9".
You may recognize this to be true but may have honestly and appropriately
rated yourself lower on many of the statements. If that is the case, then
rewrite the statements so that you could honestly respond with a nine.
What are your assumptions about learning and the learner?

9-5: Handling Problems of the Way: The STEER Model

Tool 5.1: Spotting Coaching Opportunities

Purpose

This form is designed to help you think about opportunities for coaching that might exist in your environment.

Directions

Use the form below to flesh out the opportunities that exist in your work environment.

- **Describe in specific behavioral terms what is happening.**
- **Describe in specific terms what the cost of the behavior is.**
- **Describe in specific terms the coaching opportunity.**

Who?	What is happening?	What is the cost?	What is the opportunity?

Tool 5.2: Diagnosing a Need

Purpose

To diagnose and understand a learning need.

Directions

Respond to each of the questions below.

What is the problem?
Does the employee know how to perform the required tasks? If No, this is a coaching opportunity.
If Yes, is there a barrier preventing the employee from performing the required tasks? If Yes, remove the barriers.
If No, does the problem still exist? If yes, then counsel the employee and apply natural consequences.

Tool 5.3: Developing a Coaching Plan

Purpose

Effective coaches are prepared. They create a plan for their coaching.

Directions

Fill out the form below for each coaching opportunity you find in your team.

Position or Job:	
Tasks Required to Execute Job:	
Needs	Tasks Required
1	
2	
3	
Step	Plan
1	
2	
3	
4	
5	
6	

Tool 5.4: Delivering Coaching

Purpose

Coaching is a process of taking in information and then using it to enable learning in another person. This activity provides you a series of checklists you can use to evaluate yourself as you engage in this process.

Directions

After each coaching engagement, evaluate yourself
(or have an observer do so).

Assessing the Learning Need		
Did the Learner --	Yes	No
Understand the task to be performed?		
Understand the scope of the task?		
Know how the task is to be performed?		
Know when the task must be completed?		
Know how well they are doing?		
Know how to perform the task to the level of competence required?		
Know of any obstacles hindering performance of the task?		
Have a positive attitude about the task?		

Spot the Training Needs and Opportunities to Meet Them		
Did You (the Coach) --	Yes	No
Get involved with the learner?		
Ask the learner what their needs are?		
Put the learner at ease?		
Listen to the learner's concerns?		
Discuss the learning opportunity?		
Use questions to further clarify the need?		
Explain the need and its importance?		

Tailor the Training to the Learner's Style		
Did You (the Coach) --	Yes	No
Arrange a time for coaching?		
Introduce the coaching action plan?		

Tailor the Training to the Learner's Style		
Discuss the rationale and objectives of the coaching process?		
Reinforce the credibility of the coaching experience?		
Explain the relevance of what was to be learned?		
Discuss how the coaching was to take place?		
Accommodate the coaching to the learner's style and needs?		

Explain and Demonstrate How the Task Should Be Done		
Did You (the Coach) --	Yes	No
Explain the larger process?		
Tell the learner what was to be done?		
Demonstrate the process?		
Model the process?		
Identify points where mistakes are likely?		
Model the correct behavior?		
Walk the learner through each step of the process?		

Encourage the Individual During Learning		
Did the Coach --	Yes	No
Stress success?		
Have the learner go through the process?		
Have learner explain each key step of the process?		
Monitor performance?		
Offer praise when warranted?		
Provide effective feedback?		
Provide ongoing encouragement?		
Correct errors immediately?		
Ask exploratory, open-ended questions?		

Review Progress During and After Completion of Learning		
Did You (the Coach) --	Yes	No
Make a plan to follow-up?		
Follow-up?		
Check to see if the coaching objective has been accomplished?		
Check with the learner to see if help is needed?		
Set a time for following-up?		
Ask the learner to perform a self-review?		
Recognize exemplary performance?		
Encourage the learner to develop a self-directed learning plan?		
Reward accomplishment?		

9-6: Handling Problems of the Will: The GUIDE Model

Tool 6.1: Attitude Problems that Need Resolving

Purpose

This tool helps you analyze problems that originate in the will and not the way.

Directions

Among your current employees, what counseling opportunities now exist? Using the form below, list each of your employees and describe behaviors that are problematic for the employee and for the team.

Employee	Behavior	Consequences of Behavior	Type of Problem: Will or Way

Tool 6.2: Diagnosing the Root Cause of the Need

What is the problem?
Does the employee know how to perform the required tasks? If No, this is a coaching opportunity.
If Yes, is there a barrier preventing the employee from performing the required tasks? If Yes, remove the barriers.
If No, does the problem still exist? If Yes, then counsel the employee and apply natural consequences.

Tool 6.3: The Counseling Checklist

Purpose

The following checklist provides an opportunity to evaluate and enhance your effectiveness in using the GUIDE process for dealing with problems of the WILL.

DIRECTIONS

The middle column lists behavioral competencies exhibited by effective coaches. For each of these competencies, use the right column to describe how you have used the competency. In the left column, rate the degree to which you are effective in performing that competency by circling the most appropriate number. Use the following scale:

1	2	3	4	5	6	7	8	9
Not at All Effective				Moderately Effective				Very Effective

THE CHECKLIST		
Skill Level	Competency	How I've Used It
1 2 3 4 5 6 7 8 9	Developing trust	
1 2 3 4 5 6 7 8 9	Communicating acceptance	
1 2 3 4 5 6 7 8 9	Acknowledging associate	
1 2 3 4 5 6 7 8 9	Exhibiting warmth	
1 2 3 4 5 6 7 8 9	Exhibiting genuineness	
1 2 3 4 5 6 7 8 9	Demonstrating concern	
1 2 3 4 5 6 7 8 9	Demonstrating caring	
1 2 3 4 5 6 7 8 9	Being responsive	
1 2 3 4 5 6 7 8 9	Being open and honest	
1 2 3 4 5 6 7 8 9	Observing performance	
1 2 3 4 5 6 7 8 9	Recognizing success	
1 2 3 4 5 6 7 8 9	Giving feedback	
1 2 3 4 5 6 7 8 9	Receiving feedback	
1 2 3 4 5 6 7 8 9	Expressing feelings	
1 2 3 4 5 6 7 8 9	Expressing needs	
1 2 3 4 5 6 7 8 9	Diagnosing problems	
1 2 3 4 5 6 7 8 9	Developing plans	
1 2 3 4 5 6 7 8 9	Creating contracts	
1 2 3 4 5 6 7 8 9	Following up	
1 2 3 4 5 6 7 8 9	Allowing natural consequences	

PROCESSING: DIAGNOSING YOUR SKILLS

As you look over your responses, answer the following questions:

1. To what extent are you satisfied with your current competency levels?

2. What are your strengths?

3. Which competencies are underdeveloped?

4. In what areas would improvement make you a more effective coach?

5. What kinds of support and resources would you need to develop these skills?

Tool 6.4: Developing the Get Better Plan

Purpose

Effective Get Better Plans are DO plans that the learner can execute without help. The following checklist provides an opportunity to evaluate and enhance your effectiveness in developing a Get Better Plan.

Directions

Rate your plans on each of the criteria below. For each NO answer, what can you do to change the plan so that it conforms to the criteria?

Is the plan	Yes	No
1. A DO plan?		
2. Specific?		
3. Behavioral?		
4. Non-contingent?		
5. Doable?		
6. Repeatable?		
Does the plan	Yes	No

7. Require a commitment of time and effort?		
8. Allow for natural consequences?		

Tool 6.5: Delivering Counseling

Purpose

Coaching is a process of taking in information and then using it to enable learning in another person. This activity provides you a series of checklists you can use to evaluate yourself as you engage in this process.

Directions

After each coaching engagement, evaluate yourself
(or have an observer do so).

Establishing Positive Involvement		
Did You (the Coach) --	Yes	No
Act with warmth?		
Use personal pronouns?		
Listen effectively?		
Focus on the learner?		
Clarify the learner's need?		

Encouraging Reflection on Current Behavior		
Did You (the Coach) --	Yes	No
Find out what the learner was doing?		
Get the learner to evaluate his or her behavior?		
Help him/her explore alternative courses of action?		
Help him/her decide to try new behaviors?		

Encouraging Reflection on Current Behavior		
Help him/her understand how their choices produced the current dilemma?		
Help him/her understand the consequences of their choices?		

Facilitating Planning		
Did the Coach --	Yes	No
Stress success?		
Clarify the relationship between values and goals?		
Help the learner define new goals?		
Help the learner develop an action plan?		
Help the learner develop a contract for change?		
Ask exploratory, open-ended questions?		

Encouraging Active Experimentation		
Did You (the Coach) ---	Yes	No
Follow-up?		
Check with the learner to see if help is needed?		
Set a time for following-up?		
Ask the learner to perform a self-review?		
Recognize exemplary performance?		
Reward accomplishment?		

Encouraging Continuous Learning		
Did You (the Coach) ---	Yes	No
Acknowledge changes?		
Provide selective approval when needed?		
Avoid criticizing or judging the learner?		

Encouraging Continuous Learning		
Ask the learner to perform a self-review?		
Recognize exemplary performance?		
Reward accomplishment?		

9-7: The High Achievement Environment

Tool 7.1: The Organizational Performance Potential Audit

Purpose

Coaching takes place in an environment. You can maximize your coaching success by creating an environment that supports performance excellence.

Directions

Circle the number that best describes your environment in relation to each item, using the scale below:

1	2	3	4	5	6	7	8	9
Not Typical		Somewhat Atypical		Moderately Typical		Typical		Very Typical

	Dimension 1: Clarity of Vision and Mission
1 2 3 4 5 6 7 8 9	1. The purpose of our work is clear and shared.
1 2 3 4 5 6 7 8 9	2. Everyone knows what the vision and mission of the team are.
1 2 3 4 5 6 7 8 9	3. There is a consensus among team members about what our vision and mission are.

| 1 2 3 4 5 6 7 8 9 | 4. We frequently discuss our vision and mission. |
| 1 2 3 4 5 6 7 8 9 | 5. The team's vision and mission is the focus of all our activities. |

Dimension 2: Clarity of Values

1 2 3 4 5 6 7 8 9	6. Team values are clearly defined.
1 2 3 4 5 6 7 8 9	7. Team members know what our values are.
1 2 3 4 5 6 7 8 9	8. Team members all share the values of the team.
1 2 3 4 5 6 7 8 9	9. Our behaviors are clearly consistent with the values of the team.
1 2 3 4 5 6 7 8 9	10. We make sure to correct behavior that is inconsistent with our values.

Dimension 3: Clarity of Mission

1 2 3 4 5 6 7 8 9	11. Every team member knows the product/service we provide and for whom.
1 2 3 4 5 6 7 8 9	12. Everyone on the team is committed to meeting customer needs and expectations.
1 2 3 4 5 6 7 8 9	13. Our shared values are compatible with our mission.
1 2 3 4 5 6 7 8 9	14. Every team member knows who our customers are.
1 2 3 4 5 6 7 8 9	15. Our customers think we are doing a good job.

Dimension 4: Clarity of Performance Goals

1 2 3 4 5 6 7 8 9	16. We have clearly defined goals and objectives.
1 2 3 4 5 6 7 8 9	17. Everyone on the team knows what she or he must do to be successful.
1 2 3 4 5 6 7 8 9	18. Our goals and objectives are consistent with our values.
1 2 3 4 5 6 7 8 9	19. We frequently discuss whether we are living up to our values.
1 2 3 4 5 6 7 8 9	20. Everyone knows how the team's goals contribute to the success of the organization.

Dimension 5: Staying Focused

1 2 3 4 5 6 7 8 9	21. There is a lot of open sharing about how to achieve team goals.
1 2 3 4 5 6 7 8 9	22. My job contributes to the success of the team.
1 2 3 4 5 6 7 8 9	23. We all work together to achieve team success.
1 2 3 4 5 6 7 8 9	24. When a problem is encountered it is resolved immediately.
1 2 3 4 5 6 7 8 9	25. Team members have clearly defined roles that clearly relate to team purposes.

Dimension 6: Ensuing Competence

1 2 3 4 5 6 7 8 9	26. My supervisor makes sure I am able to perform the work expected of me.
1 2 3 4 5 6 7 8 9	27. I have the resources I need to do my best.
1 2 3 4 5 6 7 8 9	28. I am well trained before I am expected to produce results.
1 2 3 4 5 6 7 8 9	29. I am free to do my job using the best methods available to me.
1 2 3 4 5 6 7 8 9	30. I am given many opportunities to learn and grow in my work.

Dimension 7: Providing Feedback

Rating	Item
1 2 3 4 5 6 7 8 9	31. I am well trained to accomplish the results expected of me.
1 2 3 4 5 6 7 8 9	32. I am held accountable for the results I am expected to achieve.
1 2 3 4 5 6 7 8 9	33. I get feedback about my performance on a regular basis.
1 2 3 4 5 6 7 8 9	34. The feedback I get helps me perform better.
1 2 3 4 5 6 7 8 9	35. If I make a mistake I am shown how to perform more effectively.
	Dimension 8: Motivating Team Members
1 2 3 4 5 6 7 8 9	36. Excellent performance is consistently recognized and rewarded.
1 2 3 4 5 6 7 8 9	37. I am given many opportunities for earning rewards for high performance.
1 2 3 4 5 6 7 8 9	38. The rewards I get are directly tied to the goals I am expected to achieve.
1 2 3 4 5 6 7 8 9	39. My boss expects me to perform at the highest level possible.
1 2 3 4 5 6 7 8 9	40. In our team, we identify and improve poor performance.

Scoring Grid

Record your ratings for each item and then add up the total score for each dimension.

Clarity of Vision	Clarity of Values	Clarity of Mission	Clarity of Goals
1	6	11	16
2	7	12	17
3	8	13	18
4	9	14	19
5	10	15	20
Total:	Total:	Total:	Total:
Staying Focused	Being Competent	Providing Feedback	Providing Motivation
21	26	31	36
22	27	32	37
23	28	33	38
24	29	34	39
25	30	35	40
Total:	Total:	Total:	Total:

Now plot your total scores for each dimension on the Performance Potential Profile. The height of each bar reflects the overall strength on your environment in that area.

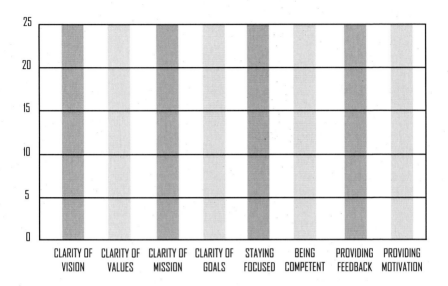

Interpretation

1. What are the most important areas of need facing the team at this time?

2. What are the consequences of this situation in terms of team functioning, problem solving and goal achievement?

3. Is this an acceptable condition at this time?

4. What changes are needed at this time?

5. What steps can you take at this time to improve the situation?

Tool 7.2: Designing Empowering Jobs

This activity will help you design jobs that empower each of your direct reports to achieve high levels of operational and safety performance.

Step 1: Defining Job Responsibilities

Job 1:
Primary Responsibilities
Job 2:
Primary Responsibilities

Step 2: Setting Goals

For each job, complete a goal matrix.

Goal Area	Results	Method	Measured By	When
Quantity				
Quality				
Time				
Interpersonal				

Step 3: Documenting Performance.

For each job, identify sources of data that will allow you to make a valid evaluation of each person's performance.

Job	Success Criteria	Data Source

Step 4: Discovering Rating Problems

Examine the jobs you are now responsible for. Identify the problems you have in providing meaningful performance feedback to your employees.

Job	Problems/Issues	Solutions

9-8: The Basics for Those in a Hurry

Tool 8.1: Personal Planning Contract Form

Purpose

To guide your development as a coach.

Directions

Complete the eight areas in the form below.

Learning Opportunity e.g., Develop my listening skills.	Coaching Skill Area e.g., Building the coaching relationship.

Needs e.g., Employees complain I don't listen.	Learning Activities e.g., Take a course on active listening.
Goals e.g., Improve employee ratings of my ability to listen actively.	Success Criteria e.g., Employee perception.
Steps	When

"Larry has truly touched the lives of our very tough and rugged oil field workforce, both at work and at home. His energy, directed towards how we can all be coaches and mentors, is contagious!"
Jeff Kinneeveauk, President | CEO, SRC Energy Services, Inc.

Larry Pearson, CSP

Larry Pearson is a professional speaker, coach and consultant. He has been recognized internationally as a passionate supporter of eliminating all workplace incidents.

As president of *The Pearson Group Inc.* in Calgary, Alberta, Canada and a Director of the *Global Safety Leaders Group*, Larry links over three decades of business leadership with the realities and challenges of today's safety leaders.

Pearson works globally helping organizations to elevate their operational safety performance and to improve the skills of their front-line leaders.

Larry's life strategy is take charge of your attitude take charge of your life. This has earned him the moniker of the "Total Attitude Guy".

If you are interested in having Larry customize a speaking event or professional development training program for your organization, you are invited to contact his Calgary office directly at:

The Pearson Group Inc.

403-271-2334

E-mail: info@totalattitude.net

www.ThePearsonGroup.ca

Keith Owen, PhD

Keith Owen, PhD brings a unique view to the subjects of individual, group and organizational change by bringing to bear his knowledge and experience of physiology and endocrinology, personality and clinical psychology, neuropsychology (Ph.D. Psychology, University of Texas at Austin), research and quantitative methods and organizational development. During his career, Dr. Owen has focused on how individuals, teams and organizations can attain and sustain high performance and excellence.

Dr. Owen has coauthored several books in this area, including *The Open Organization, Change at Work, Groups at Work, Developing the High Performance Person* and *Developing and Managing the High Performance Organization*. He has also published over 40 papers in refereed journals and other professional publications, among the most recent of which are *Creating the High Performance Culture* (Managing for Service Quality), *Making More Effective Use of Data to Promote Organizational Change* (Journal of Change Management, in press), *Creating the Service Culture* (Asia-Pacific Journal of Quality) and *Leadership Practice and Work Unit Results* (in press).

Dr. Owen has also created the *HSE Culture Opinion Survey*, the *Safety Leaders Profile* and other tools related to improving health and safety in your organization. If you would be interested in having Keith work with your organization, you are invited to contact his office directly at:

The Safety Leaders Group

512-328-6492

E-mail: kowen@somersetguild.com

www.SafetyLeadersGroup.com

Ron Mundy

Ron Mundy has a B.A. in Computer Science from the University of Texas. He has been implementing organizational research and development for over 20 years. Ron's strengths include Internet application development, structuring and managing data and data collection methodology, data mining and business and product development.

Ron is an accomplished trainer, moderator and facilitator, as well as being a partner in Somerset Consulting Group, Austin. Ron enjoys boating and is addicted to SCUBA diving.

If you are interested in contacting Ron directly, you can find him at:

The Safety Leaders Group

512-328-6492

E-mail: ron@somersetcg.com

www.SafetyLeadersGroup.com

Bibliography

Gibb, Jack. **Trust: A New View of Personal and Organizational Development.** The Guild of Tutors Press 1978

Kolb, D. A. **Experiential Learning.** Englewood Cliffs, NJ: Prentice Hall, 1984.

Luft, Joseph. **Of Human Interaction.** Palo Alto, CA: National Press, 1969.

Mink Owen and Mink. **Developing High Performance People: The Art of Coaching.** Basic Books, 1993.

Mink, Mink and Owen **Groups at Work.** Educational Technology Publications. Englewood Cliffs, New Jersey, U.S.A., 1987.

Peter Block. **The Answer to How Is Yes: Acting on What Matters.** Berrett-Koehler Publishers, 2001

The Language of DISC. Target Training International, Phoenix, Arizona.

The DNA of Safety Meetings

Over the past several years, most industries have made remarkable progress in safe work performance. Organizations have focused on equipment improvements, methods for recognizing and managing risk, educating and training people on acceptable work procedures and so on. Unfortunately, even with all of these efforts, there continues to be far too many workers injured on the job.

In writing the DNA of Safety Meetings, we asked individuals from virtually every industry what critical improvements would have the greatest impact on safer work. In almost every case, improved safety meetings were in the top category of "needs to improve" factors.

The purpose of this book is quite simple. We felt that if we could help people bridge some of the gaps and break down some of the barriers to running a successful safety meeting, we just might improve the entire worker safety environment. The book, therefore, is designed to be used in the workplace every time there is a meeting.

For more information or to obtain a copy, visit www.ThePearsonGroup.ca or the Coaching Resources Website (www.coaching-dna.com).